MW01004136

Dave Hickman has [written this?]
book is a clarion cal[l to the heart of?]
our faith: Christ *in* us. As practical and personal as it is
theological, *Closer Than Close* paints a powerful picture
of how rich and full life can be when we choose to live
out of our *in*-ness.

> **JARRETT STEVENS**
> Pastor of Soul City Church, author of *Four Small Words*

Dave Hickman has written an empowering work that
challenges us to stop trying to *earn* intimacy with God.
Our greatest freedom lies in believing that Christ offers us a
fully intimate *union* with God—an opportunity to live into
our identity as "fully loved" sons and daughters. If you find
yourself in the endless cycle of striving and trying to work
for a closer relationship with Christ, you should read this
book!

> **KEVIN PALAU**
> President of the Luis Palau Association, author of *Unlikely: Setting Aside
> Our Differences to Live Out the Gospel*

Dave Hickman reconnects us with Christianity's deepest
longing—"that all might be one . . . I in them and you in
me!" Dave reveals his heart to us, and in it we see ourselves.
Enjoy his journey, the journey of the church, and our own
invitation from Christ to be *Closer Than Close*.

> **FR. MICHAEL T. MARTIN**
> OFM Conv., director of Duke Catholic Center

While the topic of union with Christ has been engaged at the academic level, I've hoped all the while that someone would make this important truth accessible to all Christians. Dave Hickman has done just that. With wit and keen intellect, Hickman moves us from the fact of our union with Christ to living out the reality of our union with Christ. May Christians no longer strive for a Jesus "out there" but instead realize his presence within our midst.

**CHARLES RAITH II**
Assistant professor of religion and philosophy, John Brown University

For a generation searching for something more authentic, something less superficial, and something of greater depth and purpose in their faith, Dave Hickman reminds us what the gospel is truly about and invites readers to come *Closer Than Close*.

**ELISABETH NESBIT-SBANOTTO**
Assistant professor of counseling, Denver Seminary

Dave Hickman possesses keen insight into deep truth and has a remarkable ability to make clear what all Christians need to know to grow up into union with Christ, which is so much more than escaping judgment by praying a simple, one-time prayer. This is a fine, well-written, and most welcome book.

**JOHN H. ARMSTRONG**
President, ACT3 Network

"Union with Christ" is a strange and potentially scary topic to many Christians. What most of us need is not a theologian's detailed analysis, but the heartfelt reflections of a fellow Christian pilgrim, describing his own journey into the Christian faith's deepest mystery and most foundational truth. Dave Hickman is such a pilgrim, and his winsome, funny, and touching story will help you to grasp the glorious freedom that comes from knowing you are united to Christ.

DONALD FAIRBAIRN
Author of *Life in the Trinity*

# CLOSER than CLOSE

*Awakening to the Freedom*
*of Your Union with Christ*

## DAVE HICKMAN

**NavPress**

A NavPress resource published in alliance
with Tyndale House Publishers, Inc.

NavPress is the publishing ministry of The Navigators, an international Christian organization and leader in personal spiritual development. NavPress is committed to helping people grow spiritually and enjoy lives of meaning and hope through personal and group resources that are biblically rooted, culturally relevant, and highly practical.

**For more information, visit www.NavPress.com.**

*Closer Than Close: Awakening to the Freedom of Your Union with Christ*

Copyright © 2016 by David Hickman. All rights reserved.

A NavPress resource published in alliance with Tyndale House Publishers, Inc.

*NAVPRESS*, the NAVPRESS logo, *THE MESSAGE*, and THE MESSAGE logo are registered trademarks of NavPress, The Navigators, Colorado Springs, CO. *TYNDALE* is a registered trademark of Tyndale House Publishers, Inc. Absence of ® in connection with marks of NavPress or other parties does not indicate an absence of registration of those marks.

Cover photograph copyright © Eva Plevier/Stocksy.com. All rights reserved.

Author photograph by Rachel Hendrick, copyright © 2016. All rights reserved.

Published in association with the literary agency of Wolgemuth & Associates, Inc.

The Team: Don Pape, Publisher, David Zimmerman, Acquiring Editor, Ron Kaufmann, Designer

Lyrics to "Brand New Day" copyright © 2008 Joshua Radin. Used by permission.

Unless otherwise indicated, all Scripture quotations are taken from *The Holy Bible*, English Standard Version® (ESV®), copyright © 2001 by Crossway, a publishing ministry of Good News Publishers. Used by permission. All rights reserved.

Scripture quotations marked MSG are taken from *THE MESSAGE* by Eugene H. Peterson, copyright © 1993, 1994, 1995, 1996, 2000, 2001, 2002. Used by permission of NavPress Publishing Group. All rights reserved.

Scripture quotations marked NASB are taken from the New American Standard Bible,® copyright © 1960, 1962, 1963, 1968, 1971, 1972, 1973, 1975, 1977, 1995 by The Lockman Foundation. Used by permission.

Scripture quotations marked NIV are taken from the Holy Bible, *New International Version*,® *NIV*.® Copyright © 1973, 1978, 1984, 2011 by Biblica, Inc.® (Some quotations may be from the earlier NIV edition, copyright © 1984.) Used by permission. All rights reserved worldwide.

Some of the anecdotal illustrations in this book are true to life and are included with the permission of the persons involved. All other illustrations are composites of real situations, and any resemblance to people living or dead is coincidental.

**Library of Congress Cataloging-in-Publication Data**

Names: Hickman, David, date, author.
Title: Closer than close : awakening to the freedom of your union with Christ / David Hickman.
Description: Colorado Springs, CO. : NavPress, [2016] | Includes bibliographical references. | Description based on print version record and CIP data provided by publisher; resource not viewed.
Identifiers: LCCN 2016017888 (print) | LCCN 2016015621 (ebook) | ISBN 9781631464119 (Apple) | ISBN 9781631464096 (E-Pub) | ISBN 9781631464102 ( Kindle) | ISBN 9781631464089
Subjects: LCSH: Spirituality—Christianity. | Christian life.
Classification: LCC BV4501.3 (print) | LCC BV4501.3 .H523 2016 (ebook) | DDC 231.7—dc23
LC record available at https://lccn.loc.gov/2016017888

Printed in the United States of America

| 22 | 21 | 20 | 19 | 18 | 17 | 16 |
|----|----|----|----|----|----|----|
| 7  | 6  | 5  | 4  | 3  | 2  | 1  |

*For my parents, Jack and Faye Hickman*

# CONTENTS

# FOREWORD

*CLOSER THAN CLOSE* is simply extraordinary.

This is mostly because of Dave Hickman's raw honesty about his years spent huffing and puffing to get closer to God, coupled with his startling insights into the mystery of God living in us. Dave's writing is powerful because it comes out of deep personal experience, which he courageously shares. Then, in an exceptionally practical and compassionate manner, he offers hopeful and helpful practices that can lead readers into an ongoing deepening awareness, appreciation, and enjoyment of God's ever-now presence in their lives.

In this achingly bold and beautiful book, Dave tells my story (perhaps your story too) by sharing his own. After nearly two decades of relentless striving and straining to gain a sense of growing closeness to God, he felt an increasing distance. He writes, "Even though I was 'saved,' I felt lost." It was not until his world had begun to fall apart that Dave realized he'd always been as close to Jesus as he could get.

Long after Dave was first united with Christ, beneath the

veneer of his life lay weariness, discouragement, confusion, disappointment, and unresolved longing. Feeling orphaned in his relationship with God caused Dave to become less human and humane. Misunderstood and misapplied biblical truths damaged his closest relationships and kept him from experiencing his union with the God of his deepest longings.

It was the persistent urging of a mutual friend that led Dave to reach out to me for help. Despite my knowing that his life was spinning out of control, our initial encounter was more unsettling than I had anticipated. Immediately after he was seated in the cozy, quiet confines of my study, he nervously explained the cause for his sudden, brief, and repetitive movements that already were threatening my ability to listen.

Diagnosed with Tourette's syndrome in the fourth grade, Dave had also suffered the debilitating effects of obsessive-compulsive disorder, attention-deficit disorder, and anxiety and depression. Ever since, he had lived with an impending sense of doom. While asleep, he would sweat profusely. Upon waking, he suffered from "anxiety-induced vomiting." For years he dreaded nighttime and despised the coming of morning even more. Yet most devastating were the secrets he kept about himself. Eventually he led me into the hidden harbors of his heart, where fear, insecurity, and discontent had dropped anchor, revealing how his sense of identity had been tethered to externals, causing his sense of self-worth to be continually endangered.

Dave's scorching honesty and humble transparency ravished my heart and brought me to tears. Despite the severity of his physical and emotional struggles, what had most plagued him was his soul's desperate search for what he'd already been given. Clearly, the greatest discovery of his life was when Dave woke up to the truth that he had been perfectly one with Christ since the day he gave his life to Christ.

The radical transformation that has occurred in Dave's own life is what struck me most while reading *Closer Than Close*. He writes as a man who has been ambushed and held captive by the consuming fire of God's love. It is a love, Dave writes, "that crossed all boundaries not just to be close to you, but to be closer than close."

Conveying more than information to the rational mind, Dave's words are a Spirit-infused revelation to the soul. Though every follower of Jesus knows that God loves her or him, that truth often remains *a belief we hold* instead of *a belief that holds us*. Until the truth of our union with God gets into our heart, it remains information. However, once it makes its way into our heart, it brings about transformation.

Dave's life echoes a profound truth: Only the person who has experienced the love of God really knows what the love of God is; and once you have experienced it, nothing else will ever seem more beautiful and desirable. If you plan on reading just one book this year about your life with God, this is the book that you must read. I would suggest that you not just read it, but pray over each page, as I have done.

*Closer Than Close* heralds the matchless, liberating truth that God's intended home is our heart, and that it's meeting God in our depths, where God has always been, that truly transforms us from the inside out.

*Fil Anderson*
*Pastor, spiritual director, and author of* Running on Empty

# A WORD BEFORE

THIS IS A BOOK I would like to have written twenty or thirty years from now. The truth of Christ *in* us and our being *in* Christ (see John 14:20) is a profound mystery. It's one that has captured the imaginations of countless believers throughout the centuries and has been the subject of many theological conversations and debates within the church (ancient and present). In my late thirties, I am new to the conversation. Those who have devoted their lives to the study of our union with Christ will certainly notice that a novice has somehow wandered into their ranks.

While I'm not an expert in the field, however, I am someone who has personally experienced the mysterious (and freeing) reality of what it means to be united to Christ. After years of striving to be close to Jesus, I stumbled upon the shocking reality that Jesus was already as close to me as he could possibly get. It was then that I discovered, in the words of Philip Yancey, "the Jesus I never knew."[1] Striving was replaced with abiding. Guilt gave way to joy. Fear was consumed by perfect love. Awakened to my union with Christ, I have become a better and more loving husband, father, and pastor—as well as human being! While I'm not perfect, the truth of my union with Christ has *radically* changed me and continues to transform me every single day.

Our timing is not always God's timing. And for whatever the reason, now is the time to share with you my story and my current understanding of the One who desires nothing less than to be "one" with those he loves. I pray God, in his time, will use this book to gently guide you into the life-giving awareness of what is *already* true of you in Christ. In doing so, may you discover the freedom and the wonder of the ever-now reality of your union with God the Father, Son, and Holy Spirit.

Broadly speaking, I offer this book as my labor of love to the evangelical church of which I'm proudly a part. I hope that her leaders, pastors, and members will read this book with the heart in which I have written it—a heart bursting with love and optimism. It's exciting to see many within my tradition beginning to reimagine faith and practice through the lens of the early church and uniting around the affirmations of the ancient creeds. In doing so, I am confident that the evangelical church will continue to experience refreshing times of renewal and reform in the years ahead.

The pages that follow contain my heart and soul. They represent my best attempt to articulate in everyday language one of the greatest discoveries of my life. As you read and interact with these pages, may our heavenly Father grant you a fresh awareness of his love and formulate a new vision for your participation in Christ's body—the church.

# ACKNOWLEDGMENTS

MANY HAVE HELD ME under the arms and supported me as I have walked the long road of turning these hopes and prayers into the book you hold.

To Jack and Faye Hickman, thank you for modeling the undying and illogical love of God over the years. I'm honored to be called your son. Also to my sister, Amy. Thank you for always being there if (and when) I need you.

To Mike Moses Sr., thank you for sitting with me every week for a year, hearing my story, and helping me work through so much of my personal and religious baggage. To Fil Anderson, thank you for your tears. It was your tears more than your words that awakened me to the deep union I already had with Christ but was unable to see. Thank you.

To Charles Raith, Dave Nelson, Rob Kelly, John Armstrong, Stephen Copeland, Ross Chapman, Joseph Phillips, Rick Daley, Jeff Jackson, and my Franciscan friend Fr. Louis "Louie" Canino, thank you for sitting with me and providing me with laughter, comfort, and reassurance that this book could (and should) happen. Most of all, thank you for being my friends. A special thanks to Andrew Wolgemuth and the team at Wolgemuth & Associates. Thank you for believing in me at a time when I was starting to lose belief in myself. Also to NavPress, and specifically David "The Wizard" Zimmerman, my editor and new friend. Thank you for your excitement, support, and wizardry on the manuscript. I'm beyond grateful for the opportunity to be part of your growing family of authors.

I'm indebted to my friend Donald Fairbairn, whose own book on the subject, *Life in the Trinity*, served as the clarifying work for the book. To Robert Letham, J. Todd Billings, Marcus Peter Johnson, and Michael Reeves, I could not and would not have been able to write this book without your own writings on the subject. I hope this book will be a subtle primer for others to dive headlong into your much more thorough and complete works on the mystery we have come to love.

I'd be remiss not to mention the many artists whose music comforted me as I wrote late at night. To Noah Gundersen; Joshua Radin; Iron and Wine; Lord Huron; M83; S. Carey; Bon Iver; and the duo from Bozeman, Montana—Storyhill. Thank you for keeping my humanity before me while I wrestled with ideas of divinity.

Finally, to my family. Monica, my bride, thank you for loving me with an unrelenting, unbridled, everlasting love. Thank you for your patience and your grace over the last year. I love being one with you. To my three boys, Ryan,

Cole, and Jack. Your father is proud of you. I'm infinitely happy and fully pleased with who you are and who you are becoming. I pray that one day you will read this book and fall more in love with Jesus as you come to awaken to and marvel at your own union with Christ and his bride, the church.

*I will not leave you as orphans;*
*I will come to you. . . .*

*In that day you will know that I am in my*
*Father, and you in me, and I in you.*

—JESUS (JOHN 14:18, 20)

# THE WHITE ARROW

You would think after a lifetime of seeing it I would have recognized it. But I admit, I had no idea there was anything more than the bold lettering and the vibrant colors. But there is more, much more.

Embedded within the FedEx logo is something so unique that many people consider it to be the single most important aspect of the entire design. Because of it, the FedEx logo has won over forty major design awards and was named by *Rolling Stone* magazine as one of the eight best logos of the last thirty-five years.[1] Yet, for the first thirty-six years of my life, I remained completely oblivious to its existence.

Do you know what it is? If not, don't feel bad. I just found out about it a few months ago. Let me give you a hint. It's located between the *E* and the *x*.

For those of you whispering, "A white arrow," congratulations. You must be one of the chosen ones (or you work for FedEx).

The first time a friend pointed the white arrow out to me,

I remember being shocked (and a little embarrassed). *How could something so obvious and so blatant escape my attention all these years?* But now, every time a FedEx truck drives by, every time I receive a package, the white arrow is the first thing I see. In many ways, it's the only thing I see.

—

You would think after close to thirty years of being a Christian, I would have put two and two together. But I'll be the first to admit, I had no clue there was anything more to the gospel than salvation by grace, forgiveness of sins, and the ability to have a personal relationship with Jesus. Vibrant realities, sure, but that was all I saw.

Although I had read large portions of the Bible, received two degrees in theology, and listened to countless sermons regarding the nature of salvation, I remained strangely unaware of what many of my colleagues (and people throughout the centuries) have celebrated as *the* central aspect of the entire Christian faith. You can imagine my astonishment (and slight embarrassment) when an unlikely teacher pointed it out to me a few years back. But now that I've seen it, I consider it to be not only the centerpiece of the gospel but also the "glue" that binds the entire story of God together in a unified way.

Do you know what it is? Let me give you a hint. It's illustrated throughout the Bible as the relationship food and water have with the body, a building has with its foundation, a vine has with its branches, and a husband has with his wife. You can see glimpses of it between Genesis and Malachi, but it particularly stands out in the writings of the New Testament—especially the Gospel of John and writings of the apostle Paul. So, what is this mysterious part of the gospel? See if *you* can spot it in the words of Jesus below:

> I will not leave you as orphans; I will come to you.
> . . . In that day you will know that I am in my
> Father, and you in me, and I in you.
> JOHN 14:18, 20

Did you see it? Like the white arrow, it's easy to miss. Yes, it involves the word *in*. But keep going. Here's a nudge: If something (or someone) is "in" another person, we say those two are in [blank] with each other.

*Relationship?* Right. But not close enough.

*Harmony?* Closer. But still not there yet.

*Union?* Ahh! Now we're seeing!

To be "in" someone and have that someone "in" us isn't just close, it's closer than close—it's to be in "union" or "one-ness" with that person. Embedded in Jesus' words above lies, in the fiery words of the late Brennan Manning, the scandalous promise

> that the living God seeks more than an intimate
> relationship with us. The reckless, raging fury of
> Yahweh culminates, dare we say it, in a symbiotic

fusion, a union so substantive that the apostle Paul would write: "IT IS NO LONGER I WHO LIVE, BUT CHRIST LIVES IN ME."[2]

—

When I was growing up in the evangelical South, words such as *union* and *oneness* were rarely (if ever) used in relation to the gospel. Instead, the focus of the faith rested firmly on entering into a "relationship" with Jesus, whereby we could benefit from his "finished work on the cross"—benefits such as eternal life, forgiveness of sins, and a right standing (or status) before God. To claim to be "united" to Christ would have been looked upon with a fair amount of suspicion and associated more with "new ageism" or Eastern mysticism than "biblical" Christianity. It drew dangerously close to the clear line that separated Christ's divinity from our humanity.

But it turns out that union with Christ has long been considered to be the central message of the gospel. John Murray, long-standing professor of systematic theology at Westminster Theological Seminary, contends,

*Nothing* is more central or basic than union and communion with Christ. . . . Union with Christ is really the *central truth* of the whole doctrine of salvation not only in its application but also in its once-for-all accomplishment in the finished work of Christ.[3]

John Calvin, in his *Institutes of the Christian Religion*, affirms Murray's words: "For we await salvation from him [Christ] not because he appears to us afar off, but because he makes us, *ingrafted into his body*, participants not only in all his benefits but also in himself."[4]

But what does union with Christ mean? *How* are believers united to Christ in such a way that we are made "one" with him and "ingrafted into his body"? And more importantly, what difference does it make to understand salvation as "union and communion with Christ"? Aren't we saved by grace through faith?

While union with Christ, as a profound mystery (see Ephesians 5:32), cannot be fully *comprehended*, I am convinced that ordinary people like you and me can be *apprehended* by its reality in our lives. And as believers in Jesus Christ, we should be. Actually, we *have* to be. For to live oblivious of this truth is equivalent to a spouse being unaware that marriage is a union, or a boy never realizing there is such a thing as "sonship." Becoming conscious of our union with Christ is imperative for a full understanding of God, self, salvation, and the depths of God's eternal love and acceptance.

—

This book is an attempt not to offer something "fresh" or "new" but to offer hope and healing to all who need a new and fresh awareness of Jesus in their lives. This book is for everyday people who sit in pews and padded seats on Sunday mornings, yearning to experience Jesus in a deeper way but feeling "stuck" in their faith. This book is for those who haven't been to church in years and even for those who have thrown in the towel on trying to follow Jesus altogether. But most of all, this book is for anyone who feels tired, exhausted, skeptical, discouraged, and orphaned in his or her relationship with Christ. If any of these words describe you, may the gentle and inclusive words of Jean Vanier encourage you:

> [The holiness that comes from union with Christ] is
> not reserved for those who are well-known mystics
> or for those who do wonderful things for the poor.
> [It] is for all those who are poor enough to welcome
> Jesus. It is for people living ordinary lives and who
> feel lonely. It is for all those who are old, sick,
> hospitalized or out of work, who open their hearts in
> trust to Jesus and cry out for his healing love.[5]

No matter who you are, what you've done, or how close you presently feel to Jesus, you can awaken to the mind-blowing reality of your union with Christ and experience its life-altering power. No matter if you've been a Christian for fifty years or a few weeks, awakening to your union with Christ will allow you to discover the intimacy with Jesus you've always longed for, and the type of life you've always wanted to live—a life overflowing with the fruits of union with Christ, fruits such as love, joy, peace, and patience. As you read, I pray you will begin to view yourself, your relationships, the spiritual disciplines, and Christ's mission (locally and globally) in a whole new light. Most of all, I hope you will find rest for your well-worn soul. Instead of endlessly "chasing after God" and perpetually trying to "press into" the heart of Jesus, may you discover the mind-bending truth that you are already as close to God as you can possibly get—having been made one with him in Christ.

Brennan Manning once suggested that "the real dichotomy in the Christian community today is not between conservatives and liberals or creationists and evolutionists but between the awake and the asleep."[6] Truer words have never been spoken. As you read, my personal plea to the Father is that the Holy Spirit will open your eyes and graciously allow you to awaken to the overwhelming and scandalous love that God the Father, God the Son, and God the Holy Spirit *already* has for you in Christ Jesus—a love that crossed all boundaries not just to be close to you, but to be closer than close.

# 1

## STRIVING TO ABIDE

*Just a closer walk with Thee,*
*Grant it, Jesus, is my plea,*
*Daily walking close to Thee,*
*Let it be, dear Lord, let it be.*

AUTHOR UNKNOWN

I BEGAN A RELATIONSHIP with Jesus between third and fourth grade. It was 1986—the year of Hulk Hogan, Garbage Pail Kids, and Chuck Norris action figures. Ronald "Ray-Gun" was president, gas was eighty-nine cents a gallon, and *Top Gun* was a box-office smash. I had a mad crush on the lead singer of the Bangles, and "Walk This Way" by Aerosmith and Run-DMC was my favorite song. I remember being heartbroken when David Lee Roth was "booted" from Van Halen and sitting horrified as I watched the space shuttle *Challenger* explode into a ball of flames on our wooden floor-model television.

One evening that summer I was sitting in the living room with my older sister, Amy, waiting on our parents to take us to Sunday evening service at church. Growing up in the hills of East Tennessee, everybody seemed to go to some flavor of Baptist church. There were Missionary Baptists; Primitive Baptists; Southern Baptists; Independent Baptists; Full Gospel Baptists; First, Second, and Third Baptists; and what we were—Freewill Baptists.

Most Sundays, our family would go to church in the morning and again that night. Sometimes we would go on Wednesday evenings as well, which seemed to cap off the spiritual trifecta of the week. While I heard a lot about God and Jesus when I was a kid, I never fathomed that either one (or both) wanted much to do with me. The times I did think about them (which wasn't very often), I pictured two misty figures floating around in heaven somewhere ensuring that I was "safe from harm" and "being a good boy." As for the Holy Spirit? Well, I didn't think about him at all; no one talked about him much. Having seen *Return of the Jedi*, I figured I knew everything I needed to know about the Holy Force—I mean, Holy Spirit.

I believed that God and Jesus loved me. But I also believed that they were strict and stern—critical, even. In many ways, I pictured them like Statler and Waldorf from *The Muppet Show*, two grumpy old guys eternally peering down on my life, shaking their holy heads in constant disapproval.

**God:** Look at that Dave Hickman down there. Boy, he's not half bad, is he?

**Jesus:** Nope . . . he's *all* bad!
**Both:** BAAAHAHAHAHAHAHA!

But a few weeks earlier, my sister had "asked Jesus into her heart." And now God and Jesus seemed as real to her as her right and left arm.

**Amy:** Dave, does Jesus live in your heart?
**Me:** Huh?
**Amy:** Okay, go to your room, close the door, get on
   your knees, and ask Jesus to come into your heart.
**Me:** Okay.

I wasn't sure what closing the door behind me and getting on my knees had to do with anything, but I did *exactly* as Amy said. I knelt beside my bed and humbly prayed, "Jesus, come into my heart." I meant every word, even though my prayer was so brief it felt more like a magical phrase—like "abracadabra" or "alakazoo." In my mind's eye, though, I envisioned the pasty-white, long-haired Jesus from the cover of my children's Bible open my heart with his hands and slide in, one foot at a time.

It was in that moment that God and Jesus took me by surprise. To quote the famous words of John Wesley, my heart suddenly became "strangely warmed." I found myself overcome with a mysterious and compassionate love I had never experienced. It was deep, real, and true. While I didn't know all the theology surrounding sin and salvation,

I knew from that moment on that somehow Jesus lived in my heart.

## BOUND AND DETERMINED

On that sultry summer evening in 1986, I began what I would later learn to call a "relationship" with Jesus. I later discovered, however, that having a relationship with Jesus was only the *first step* in the Christian journey. According to my youth pastor, the *overarching goal* of the Christian life was to establish a "close and personal" relationship with Jesus, and that could only come about with time.

Although "close" and "personal" were never really defined (and strangely subjective), one thing was clear: In order to be close to Jesus, I needed to do certain things—things like praying, reading the Bible, and regularly attending church. Most of all, I needed to do the things I should and not do the things I shouldn't. According to my youth pastor (and most sermons I heard back then), the more faithful and committed I was to these things, the closer I could get to Jesus.

I became bound and determined to be as close to Jesus as humanly possible. I would wake up an hour before school, run down into the den of my parents' house, and listen to the music of Steven Curtis Chapman and DC Talk before having my "quiet time." I prayed using the well-known acrostic ACTS, which stands for "Adoration," "Confession," "Thanksgiving," and "Supplication." And every time the church doors were open, I was in the front row with the rest of the youth group singing my heart out.

I was so determined to be close to Jesus that I eventually threw away all of my '90s hip-hop CDs (a decision I would later deeply regret), quit going to R-rated movies, and made a promise not to have sex before I was married. I did all of this willingly and joyfully out of my love for Jesus and my insatiable desire to draw close (and remain close) to the God I loved.

By the time I entered high school, I was "on fire" for Jesus. I became the president of our local chapter of the Fellowship of Christian Athletes and took on additional leadership roles within my church. I read every Max Lucado book there was, and worked through *The Mind of Christ* by T. W. Hunt and Claude V. King twice. I was a spiritual beast. Jesus was as close to me as I was to myself back then. I was head over heels in love with him.

Most of all, I was convinced that Jesus was head over heels in love with me. I mean, how could he not be? I had done everything I knew to do to please him and draw close to him. Little did I know that in a few short years, what seemed like closeness would feel like a great distance.

## DETERMINED AND BOUND

College. I went there to study theology. I also went there to play baseball. I had a passion for both and wanted to attend a school where I could play the game I loved and grow in my faith in the process. Although I received multiple offers from local universities around Tennessee, I decided to go to Montreat College, a Presbyterian school up the road from the small town of Black Mountain, North Carolina. Because of its Bible and Religion program and impressive baseball team, I was convinced that Montreat would be a perfect place to draw closer to Jesus than ever before.

For the first semester, it was. But over time, I became preoccupied with other things: writing theology papers, dating, and playing *Mario Kart* into the wee hours of the morning. Instead of waking up early to read my Bible and pray before class, I would drag myself out of bed in a puffy-eyed fog, throw on a pair of sweatpants, and stagger into my classroom. I would normally fall back asleep before the professor even entered the room. I still wanted to stay close to Jesus, but with every morning that I skipped my devotions, I felt as if I was drifting further and further from him.

As for not doing things I shouldn't? That became a lot harder as well. Things I promised myself (and God) I would never do, I found myself doing. And doing again. And again. And then again. Although I was learning more about Jesus and wanted desperately to please and obey him, I became trapped in what seemed to be an endless cycle of sin–confession–sin–confession–sin–confession. Before long, the peaceful quiet times I used to enjoy were replaced by panicked pleas for God to forgive me of my failures the night before. Eventually, my desire to spend time with Jesus started to fade altogether as I found myself perpetually "hung over" with a lingering sense of guilt and self-condemnation.

By my sophomore year, I couldn't shake the feeling that my proximity to Jesus was somehow contingent on the faithfulness of my spiritual devotion. What I mean is, when I was consistent in praying, reading the Bible, and doing as I should, I considered myself to be "close" to Jesus. When I failed to do these things (which most often was the case), I thought myself to be "far" from him.

Before long, I became consumed with the fear of falling out of a relationship with Jesus altogether—which, consequently, only served to make me strive even harder to draw close (and remain close) to Jesus through *more* discipline, *more* study, and *more* good works. Ironically, the more determined I became, the more bound I found myself—bound by guilt, frustration, and self-condemnation. Even during the times I was able to check all the boxes on my spiritual "to do" list, there remained a strange nagging deep in my soul—a mysterious discontentedness about my relationship with Jesus. I was caught between wanting to please Jesus and not being able to. I jostled between feeling far from Jesus when I *wasn't* doing as I should, and longing to be closer still when I *was*. My life resembled the words of the apostle Paul in Romans:

> I do not understand what I do. For what I want to
> do I do not do, but what I hate I do. . . . In my inner
> being I delight in God's law; but I see another law at
> work in me, waging war against the law of my mind
> and making me a prisoner of the law of sin at work

within me. What a wretched man I am! Who will
rescue me from this body that is subject to death?

ROMANS 7:15, 22-24, NIV

At night in my dorm room, I would plead with Jesus to
deliver me from the prison of sin and apathy I found myself
in, and draw me close to him again. But no matter how ear-
nestly I prayed, I continued to wrestle with sin at night and
drag out of bed in the morning. And Jesus seemed to be a
million miles away.

## GONE WITH THE WIND

I wish I could tell you that somewhere between college, getting married, and becoming an "adult," the distance between
Jesus and me closed. It didn't. If anything, the space between
us continued to grow. Marriage, paying bills, and earning a
living depleted my emotional reserves, making reading my
Bible and praying that much more difficult. But I didn't give
up. No sir. I continued to fight for my relationship with
Jesus. How could I not? To give up was incomprehensible.
*How could I give up on the one relationship that was supposed
to save me?*

Desperate, I joined a small group at my church. I scoured
Amazon and Barnes & Noble, crossing my fingers to stumble
upon that irresistible devotional (you know, the one with a
good cover). I attended Christian conferences and events,
praying (and paying) to press into the heart of God. I even
purchased a diary (excuse me, journal) to record my feelings!

While all of these were helpful, *none of them* (not even going to church) bridged the gap for good. Jesus remained as elusive as ever, leaving me perpetually grasping for him like a child chasing a balloon in the wind.

I expressed my frustrations one evening in my journal:

> *Jesus,*
> *What is wrong with me? What is wrong with us?*
> *Why do I feel so distant from you? Why do you seem so*
> *distant from me? I've done everything I know to do to*
> *be close to you. Yet, why does my heart long for more*
> *and my soul yearn for something it can't explain? Why*
> *am I constantly dissatisfied? Why am I always striving?*
> *Draw me close to you again, please. Reveal yourself and*
> *make yourself real to me, I pray.*

I wrote that entry in June 2003—seventeen years after beginning a relationship with Jesus. As I wrote it, I remember reminiscing on the spiritual bliss of my middle school and high school years. Actually, I've lived the large majority of my life in the shadow of that faithful, devoted little boy. The one who used to sing loud and mean it. The one who used to pursue Jesus with all his heart. The one who used to feel close to Jesus. The one who used to know he was loved of God.

But after nearly two decades of chasing hard after Jesus, I finally lost sight of him. And in doing so, I lost sight of myself. Even though I was "saved," I felt lost. While I was a "son of God," I felt like an orphan. While everything on the outside appeared fine (because that's how Christians are sup-posed to be), on the inside I was living a life, in the words of Henry David Thoreau, of "quiet desperation."

But the wind, according to Jesus, blows wherever it pleases; you can hear its sound, but you cannot tell where it comes from or where it is going. So it is with the Spirit of God (see John 3:8). And at the most unexpected time, and through the most unlikely of ways, the Spirit of God breathed Jesus back into full view for me. And nothing could have prepared me for how close Jesus was in that moment—the moment I became a father for the first time.

## DISCUSSION QUESTIONS

1. *Describe your faith journey. When was the first time your heart became "strangely warmed" by Christ's presence?*

2. *In one word, describe your current relationship with Jesus. Why did you choose that particular word?*

3. *Describe a time when you felt particularly close to God.*

4. *The author shared that he considered his proximity to Jesus to be based on the faithfulness of his spiritual devotion (praying, reading the Bible, going to church). Do you feel this way? Have you felt this way? Explain.*

# 2

# THE BOND OF BREATH

*Then the LORD God formed the man of dust from the
ground and breathed into his nostrils the breath of
life, and the man became a living creature.*

GENESIS 2:7

*THERE IS A STRENGTH in women that is not found within
the hearts of men.* This was the thought that kept running
through my mind as I knelt between the quivering knees of
my wife in the delivery room. It had been two hours since
the doctor broke Monica's water and pumped her veins full
of Pitocin—that devilish drug that brings fast and furious
contractions for those being induced.

Our first son, Ryan, was supposed to have been born three
days earlier. However, he proved to be just as stubborn as
his mom, who had decided against taking any type of pain-
relieving drug during labor. She wasn't against the idea; she just
wanted to "see what it would be like" to have a "natural" birth.

"Are you absolutely sure?" I asked Monica for what must have been the hundredth time as we drove to the hospital that morning. "I've never heard of anybody wanting to see what 'natural' dental work would be like. Have you?" My voice was freighted with as much trepidation as sarcasm. Truth be known, I was trying to convince Monica to reduce her pain for my sake more than hers. I had Googled "natural child-birth." I had seen the grisly images and had watched the disturbing YouTube videos. I sat withered in horror during the birth scenes in movies like *Alien*, *Look Who's Talking*, and *She's Having a Baby*. I knew exactly what I was about to experience: nausea, terror, and possible loss of consciousness.

My rhetorical question was of no use, though. Like Monica's mind, the birth plan had been set months ago, leading up to this moment—the moment that would forever change the way I view my relationship with Jesus.

﹉

"On a scale of one to ten, how bad is it?" I asked in childlike wonder. Another contraction had bolted through Monica's abdomen, sending shock waves deep into her lower back and throwing her forward into my arms.

*Close*, Monica mouthed through chapped lips.

"The baby is close?" I shot back, not caring that she hadn't acknowledged my question.

"I want *you* close," she whispered, and she collapsed back into the glider for a few seconds of rest.

Ryan *was* close, it turns out. He would arrive any minute. As the doctors entered the room and began suiting up
in their blue scrubs and rubber gloves, I gently stood up
from between Monica's knees where I had been kneeling and
placed my cheek against hers so that the outside corners of
our eyes touched. This is what she meant by close. She wasn't
looking for proximity; she was looking for intimacy. There is
something about that piece of flesh located just outside the
lower eyelash. It's sensual and comforting. It was as close as
I could get to her in that moment.

With our eyelashes fluttering together, I inched my
chest closer into hers while holding a heating pad on the
small of her back. "We'll do this together," I whispered. But
before I could finish, another contraction ripped through
her body.

I tried not to panic. "Breathe, Monica. Breathe!" I coached,
and for the next several minutes, we did exactly that—we
breathed together. Our chests filled with air at the same time
and we exhaled in perfect harmony. With each contraction
we rocked back and forth in exact cadence and clung to each
other as if we were one.

"Breathe in . . . breathe out," I said gently as she relaxed.
"Breathe in . . . breathe out . . ."

In between contractions, I would sometimes kneel back
down to give my own back a rest. On one occasion, Monica's
wedding ring caught my eye. I thought about the day I
bought it and how excited (and obsessed) I was over it. I
thought about when I asked Monica to throw her life away

and become my wife. I thought about our wedding day and the vows we made to each other. I remembered the minister's words—that mysterious declaration that we were no longer two, but one. I thought about our spiritual union and how our physical union had somehow conceived the new life we were about to witness.

Where these thoughts of union were coming from, I did not know. But what I did know was that I didn't want to break from Monica when the doctor said it was time for her to move over to the bed. Ryan was moments away.

—

*Here we go*, I said to myself, terrified. *This is it*. My heart raced with anticipation and fear as the nurses helped Monica onto the bed. I held a cold washrag on her forehead. Monica gritted her teeth and pushed.

"One-two-three-four-five-six-seven-eight-nine-ten. Rest!" the doctor commanded as if redlining a motor to see if it would blow.

"You're doing great, baby. You're doing amazing." I kept a suspicious stare locked on the doctor.

"One-two-three-four-five-six—keep pushing!—seven-eight-nine-ten—Good!" the doctor revved once again. "One more big push and the baby will be here!" The doctor looked at me through her thick goggles. I knew what question was coming next. I saw the look in her eye—the look that says, *Are you ready for your mind to be blown?*

"You wanna see this?" the doctor asked with a smirk. I had already weighed the options and decided flatly against it. There are some things that are best left unknown.

"Absolutely," I said before realizing what I was doing. I handed the washrag to Monica's mom and slipped in behind the doctor. I was immediately taken aback. It was as beautiful as it was gruesome. I studied the tangled mess of humanity before me and felt as if *I* were the one in labor, as if *I* were the one being born.

*This is life*, I remember thinking. *Messy. Painful. Joyful. Exposed. Hanging in the balance.*

With one last determined push, the little boy whom I had only seen in black-and-white ultrasound pictures emerged from the womb wrapped in warm, chalky flesh. I coughed up a cry.

As the doctor sucked the goo out of Ryan's nose and mouth, I couldn't take my eyes off of my son. His wrinkly, soft hands; his frail legs; his puffy, swollen eyes; his blood-red lips; his wide-open mouth. I became possessed by a tremendous fury of love. Everything in me wanted to be as close as possible to this little boy, created in my image and after my likeness.

As I was sorting through my feelings, I thought of the old saying, "I want to eat him up." I wanted Ryan in me somehow. That's how close I wanted to be to my son. Before I knew it, I had made my way through the nurses to get to Ryan. As I held him in my arms, I did something that made absolute and complete sense to me but seemed to shock and confuse everyone else.

I stuck my nose directly in his mouth.

It was more of a reaction than anything else. I wanted to be closer than close to this little baby boy whom I had watched grow from afar in the womb of my wife. I wanted to breathe his breath into my lungs and breathe my breath back into him. I wanted us to share the same breath.

With my nose in his mouth (and the doctor looking at me like I was a madman), I closed my eyes, inhaled Ryan's breath, and then, after a moment, exhaled my breath (our breath) back into his wide-open mouth. For what felt like an eternity, we breathed in and out together as one.

Finally, I filled my lungs with one last breath, trying to burn that moment into my memory. I reluctantly exhaled, in a dizzy wonder that in some way, Ryan had been in me and I had been in him. In that instant, all of life seemed to come sharply into focus.

That's when it happened.

As I stood there gazing into Ryan's cloudy, grey eyes, I heard something from *deep* within me—a voice of sorts, coming from a part of me that I forgot (or didn't realize) existed. I know that claiming to hear a voice sounds spooky and irrational. But I heard a voice that day as clear as I've heard *anything* in my life—not audible, more like the sudden realization of a truth I had always known but was unable to identify.

*That's it, Dave. You got it.*

The voice was as gentle and carefree as a thin curtain flapping lazily in a warm summer breeze. But just as quickly as the voice came—*whoosh*—it was gone, dissipating into thin air as quickly as the breath I had exhaled moments before.

A chuckle broke through my tears as I smiled and nodded in perfect agreement with the voice.

*That's it, Dave. You got it,* I whispered over and over, staring in wonder at my newborn son.

## AWAKENING TO LOVE

That day in the delivery room, I experienced a depth of love I had only known with one other person—my bride. It was a love that transcended intimacy and obliterated proximity—a love so absolute that anything short of "union" would have been to leave my heart void of love itself. It was a love so furious that it refused to stop until it became perfectly one with the object of its affection.

That night as Monica and Ryan slept, I lay quietly (and uncomfortably) on the couch, gazing at my wife and newborn son. As I did, my imagination raced with the concept of union. Although a familiar word, it was one I rarely (if ever) used in my everyday language. But evidences of union *had* permeated my life and faith in many ways; the proof was lying right in front of me! In fact, the proof had *always been* right before my eyes; I just never stopped long enough to notice.

I thought about the "one flesh" union Monica and I shared in marriage. I thought about the union of my physical body. I thought about the union within the created order. I thought about the oneness of the triune God I learned about at Montreat. I thought about my baptism, where I was united with the death, burial, and resurrection of Jesus. I thought about Communion and the many times the bread and the wine (usually juice) had become a part of my physical body. *What if the union I longed to have with my son was but a pale reflection of a "oneness" I always longed to have with Jesus? What if Jesus never wanted to have a "close relationship" with me? What if he always wanted to be "one" with me instead?* I was captivated and troubled by these daring questions.

Falling asleep that night, I felt as if I was finally coming awake. Like the dawning of a new day, the hope of being united to Christ illuminated my soul, revealing new landscapes of a spiritual reality I never considered or knew existed. As I gazed over the foreign terrain in my mind's eye, I was captivated by the beautiful vistas of rest, peace, and acceptance. Union with Christ was unlike anything I had ever imagined. Far removed from striving, guilt, and condemnation, there were no rules, no expectations—only freedom.

Trying to picture myself united to Christ was like trying to picture eternity (or the Panthers winning a Super Bowl). It was too glorious, too grand, and too wonderful to comprehend. One of my theology professors at Montreat loved to use the word *ineffable* to describe such mysteries. I had no idea what he was talking about. So, one day, I looked it up.

That night, lying on that uncomfortable couch in the hospital, my imagination was captivated with the ineffable— and it was "too great or extreme to be expressed or described in words."[1] But, as we will see, union with Christ is not only ineffable, it's a part of a larger story—a story I refer to as the Divine Mystery.

Let me explain.

## DISCUSSION QUESTIONS

1. *When you think of the word* union, *what comes to mind? Explain.*

2. *Complete this sentence: "The thought of being united to Christ makes me feel _____." Explain your answer.*

3. *The author wrote that he was "captivated and troubled" by the concept of being united to Christ. What captivates you regarding the thought of being united to Christ? What troubles you about it?*

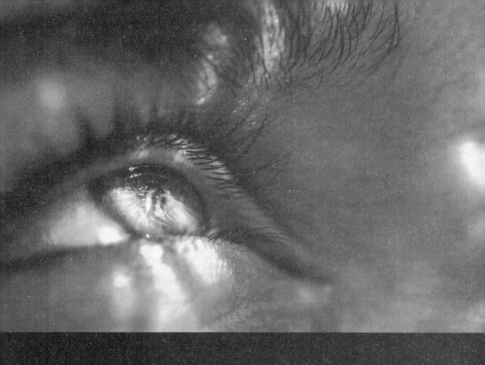

PART ONE

The Divine Mystery

# 3

# THE MYSTERY OF GOD

*To say that God is a mystery is to say that you can never nail him down.*
FREDERICK BUECHNER, *WISHFUL THINKING*

*THAT'S IT, DAVE. You got it.* But I didn't get it right away. As you probably know, one experience (no matter how profound) rarely changes you immediately. It took several years (and many more revelations) before the concept of union with Christ settled into my heart. The roots of my performance-based acceptance ran much too deep. Plus, I had no category by which to understand my relationship with Jesus as a "union." The thought short-circuited me theologically and seemed impossible practically. *How can humanity be united with divinity? Is that possible? If so, what does union with Christ actually mean?*

Before Ryan was born, I started to feel a bit better about

my relationship with Jesus. I had just enrolled at Gordon-Conwell Theological Seminary in Charlotte, where I was learning to systematize my faith and order my thoughts about the nature of salvation. But just as I was about to figure God out, he became more mysterious than ever. Any confidence and security I gained quickly faded into mystery and wonder as I became captured by the possibility of humanity becoming "one" with God.

I wish I had the space to share with you all the ways God continued to draw me into the deep mystery and bright reality of my union with him. But those stories will have to wait for now. I imagine you are curious as to what union might actually mean as well. I understand. But before we can answer that, we first have to do a little groundwork. Like I said, the reality of our union with Christ is wrapped up in a divine mystery—the mystery of God.

When we think of the word *mystery*, we typically think of something unknown or hidden, something we have to solve—as in the board game *Clue* or a James Patterson novel. But when the Bible uses the word *mystery*, it is most often referring not to something unknown but rather to something that has now been fully revealed. And there is no greater mystery in the entire Bible than its unfolding revelation of the union that has forever existed within God himself.[1]

## SINGULAR PLURALITY

Since the beginning of time, God has revealed himself many times and in many ways to the human race. In a general sense, all that God has created, from the smallest insect to the largest galaxy, reveals his eternal power and his divine nature (see Romans 1:20). David affirms this:

> The heavens declare the glory of God,
>     and the sky above proclaims his handiwork.
>
> PSALM 19:1

But not only has God chosen to generally reveal himself through what he has made, God has specifically made himself known to us by personally interacting and communicating with humanity. In Genesis we read how God chose a particular people (Israel) through whom to communicate the depths of his nature more fully. Part of this revelation was that God was the one true God among the false gods of the nations that surrounded them. God's supremacy is made clear in Deuteronomy 4:39: "The LORD is God in heaven above and on the earth beneath; there is no other." Probably the most well-known passage that shows God's sovereignty as well as his singularity is the *Shema*, found in Deuteronomy 6:4: "Hear, O Israel: The LORD our God, the LORD is one." In passages such as these, the biblical writers make clear that the God revealed to Israel is the one true God, and there is no other god equal to him.

But not only did Israel understand God to be sovereign, they also knew their God to be highly relational and deeply loving. This stands in *stark* contrast to the impersonal and lifeless gods of the other nations. As the one true God, Israel's

God was interested in loving and being loved. Because of this, Israel was to love the Lord God with all their heart, soul, and strength (see Deuteronomy 6:5). Throughout Israel's history, God continued to reveal his relational nature by personally communicating with, caring for, and entering into loving agreements (covenants) with his people. God also tangibly made his love known by personally appointing prophets, priests, and kings to govern and guide Israel as a nation.

By the end of the Old Testament, it was clear to the people of Israel that God was sovereign over *everything*. It was also clear that God was loving and relational. But what was not clear was the reason *why* God was loving and relational, and exactly *what type* of love defined God. And most of all, since Israel (or humanity, for that matter) didn't always exist, whom (or what) did God love before human beings?

## THE "US" OF GOD

A closer reading of the Old Testament reveals certain clues that provide an answer to these questions. For example, in Genesis 1:26, we read God saying, "Let *us* make man in our image, after *our* likeness" (emphasis added). In looking down upon the Tower of Babel, God says, "Come, let *us* go down and there confuse their language" (Genesis 11:7, emphasis added). And in Isaiah 6:8, God asks, "Whom shall I send, and who will go for *us*?"[2] It becomes evident that while God is "one," there also exists a kind of divine plurality within his singularity; enabling God to speak of himself in a singular yet plural fashion.

This "us" within the one true God of Israel remained the greatest mystery throughout the ages. Who is the "us" God is referring to in these passages? And more importantly, what *type* of relationship existed within the mysterious "us" of God? Interestingly, the Old Testament makes references to a "Son" (Psalm 2:7, 12; Isaiah 7:14; 9:6) and a "Spirit" (Genesis 1:2; Isaiah 63:10; Joel 2:28) in relation to God's nature and his being. Exactly what role (if any) this "Son" and "Spirit" played within the one God of Israel remained unclear. But the mystery surrounding God's singular plurality would one day be fully revealed.

## THE VISIBLE IMAGE OF GOD

It's not until the New Testament that the depth of God's mysterious nature comes into full focus, specifically in the Gospel according to John. In John's Gospel, we see the mystery surrounding God not only explained through written words, but personally demonstrated through the incarnation (meaning "to become flesh") of the eternal Word of God. This "Word" is described by John in the following way:

> In the beginning was the Word, and the Word was with God, and the Word was God. He was in the beginning with God. All things were made through him, and without him was not any thing made that was made. . . . And the Word became flesh and dwelt

among us, and we have seen his glory, glory as of the only Son from the Father, full of grace and truth.

JOHN 1:1-3, 14

The first chapter of John is loaded with libraries' worth of theological truths worthy of consideration. But for our purposes at this point, I'd like to highlight two that are vital for our discussion.

*The divinity of the Word.* First, John tells us that God has eternally existed in relation to "the Word." This Word was both with God in the beginning and is somehow equal to God himself. In the original language of the New Testament, "the Word" is *o logos,* and can also be translated "the speech" or "the explanation." Through this divine speech, according to John 1:3, all things were created; it is the supreme way in which God communicates his glory, grace, and truth to the world.

To reveal the nature of God (what God is like), this eternal Word, according to John, fully assumed human flesh and lived as an actual person among humanity (John 1:14). The word *flesh* commonly refers to human beings generally but also the characteristics that define one as *being* human. This divine person, who shows forth God's eternal grace and truth in the flesh, is said to be Jesus Christ himself (verses 17-18). According to John, that Jesus Christ was (and is) God the Word, who came down from heaven and lived among humanity as an actual living, breathing person.

What is stunning, however, is how the New Testament

holds firmly to Christ's absolute divinity without suggesting that Jesus and God are somehow two separate Gods.
Instead, the New Testament affirms the Old Testament
understanding of the singularity of God while showing how
God has a "Word" who is somehow the same God as he is,
not a separate God. In this way, John shows Jesus Christ to be
the incarnation of the Word, who makes visible the invisible
God (see also Colossians 1:15).

*The divinely loved Son.* John tells us not only that Jesus
is the incarnation of the eternal Word of God, but that he
eternally shares a loving *relationship* with God as his "Son"
(see John 1:14). Through Jesus Christ, the all-powerful Holy
One of Israel not only reveals himself to be the sovereign
God of the Universe; he shows himself to be an eternal *Abba*
(meaning "daddy") to the Son (Jesus Christ), who has always
existed in a familial relationship with the Father. The writer
of Hebrews affirms John's claim:

> Long ago, at many times and in many ways, God
> spoke to our fathers by the prophets, but in these
> last days he has spoken to us *by his Son*, whom he
> appointed the heir of all things, through whom also
> he created the world. He is the radiance of the glory
> of God and the exact imprint of his nature.
>
> HEBREWS 1:1-3, EMPHASIS ADDED

I'm not sure why, but for most of my Christian life, I considered the Father-Son relationship between God and Jesus to

be more metaphorical than an actual fact. Although I referred to Jesus as "God's Son," I understood the phrase to be a figurative title, or a term of endearment. But if Jesus is God's Son only in a figurative sense, then it could be argued that Jesus' claim to be *God himself* must be figurative as well. The shocking revelation of Jesus in the New Testament is that God has forever been an actual Father to an actual Son, the Word.[3]

Claiming to be equal with God was unthinkable in Jesus' day, and yet it was his insistence that God was his Father that infuriated the religious leaders to the degree that they "tried all the more" to kill Jesus (John 5:18, NIV). Claiming to have such a familial bond with the one true God of Israel was considered to be heretical—yet over and over again, Jesus insisted that he was, in fact, God's beloved Son.[4]

And if Jesus' words were not enough, twice—once at Jesus' baptism and the other at his transfiguration—God *himself* audibly affirmed the familial relationship that forever existed between the two.[5] The mystery concerning the "us" of God that had been shrouded in pillars of smoke and blazing fire throughout the Old Testament was now revealed through the person of Jesus Christ. Jesus was (and is) the Divine Word who eternally exists with the Father as his beloved Son.

## THE SPIRIT OF GOD

The mysterious nature of God does not stop with the revelation of the Word's divinity or the Father-Son relationship. Jesus "pulls back the curtain"[6] even further to reveal an equally mind-bending truth.

Remember the "Spirit" mentioned throughout the Old Testament? Well, as the New Testament unfolds, it becomes clear not only that God is a Father to a Son, but that God the Father *and* God the Son are eternally bound by a common "breath"[7] or "Spirit" who is equal to both! The exact nature of the mysterious union God the Father has with God the Son and God the Spirit, such that they constitute the one true God, has long baffled the best and the brightest of theologians. Yet it is the revelation of the three-in-one God (the Trinity) that lies at the heart of the Christian faith and separates Christianity from any other world religion.

I understand if your head is spinning at this point. Like me when my son was born, you may be taken aback by the tangled mess of divinity before you. I understand. Men and women throughout the ages have spilled rivers of ink attempting to unravel the mystery we just covered in a few short paragraphs. I also understand that many other important aspects of the Incarnation and the Trinitarian nature of God have gone unaddressed in my brief explanation. But for now, what you need to know is that the person of Jesus Christ as the Word and Son (a) fully imaged God's divine nature and (b) finally revealed the eternal truth that God has forever existed as a Father to a distinct Son, bound together as one by the Holy Spirit.

## FROM THE OUTSIDE IN

While this may be common knowledge for some of us, remember, Jesus' disciples would have known little (if any) of what we just unpacked. In fact, many of them struggled to believe *anything* Jesus said. Yet, over and over again, the disciples clearly heard Jesus claim to be God and, more frequently, the actual Son of God the Father.

Over the course of the disciples' three years with Jesus, they heard him pray to his Father (see John 17) and claim to be loved of his Father (John 10:17). They watched him joyfully doing the works of his Father (John 5:17, 36). They heard Jesus claim to be "in" the Father and that the Father was "in" him, to the degree that they were not two but "one" (John 10:30, 38). I'm not sure, but I can only imagine that the disciples must have felt a bit jealous at times of the loving bond Jesus shared with his Father. Compared to the relationship Jesus claimed to have with his own Father, the disciples must have felt like orphans. It's no wonder that on several different occasions the disciples asked Jesus to teach them how to pray to his Father (see Luke 11:1) and for Jesus to show them what his Father was like (see John 14:8).

At no point, however, would the disciples have presumed to personally share (or participate) in the loving bond that eternally exists between the two. Never. Not only would the thought have never entered their minds, but to desire such a relationship with God would bring the same persecution upon them that Jesus suffered. Even if Jesus would have offered for his disciples to somehow share in the loving relationship between he and his Father, I suspect they would have respectfully declined.

But, as they would find out, the mystery surrounding

the divine love of the Father was about to take two more unexpected turns—plot twists that would not only blow the minds of the disciples but also rock the entire world.

## DISCUSSION QUESTIONS

1. *What are some ways your view of God has changed during your life? Explain.*

2. *The author shared how he understood Jesus' claim to be God's "Son" as metaphorical instead of an actual fact. How does thinking of God as being actual Father to a real Son change the way you view God?*

3. *The Trinity of God the Father, God the Son, and God the Holy Spirit is a central truth of Christianity. How did this chapter help clarify (or complicate) your understanding of the nature of the Trinity? Explain.*

4. *The author pointed out that the disciples would have never dreamed of being included in the divine love between God the Father and God the Son. Do you think it's possible for humans to share in such an eternal and perfect love? Why or why not?*

# 4

# FAMOUS LAST WORDS

*Whenever I start getting sad about where I am in life,*
*I think about the last words of my favorite uncle: "A truck!"*

AUTHOR UNKNOWN

NOTHING CAUSES my adrenaline to run and my heart to race more than speeches that matter. For a speech to matter, words neither have to be eloquent or perfect. However, the timing has to be right. Speeches that matter come from the lips of brave men and women who dare to speak the truth at a time when other voices have withered and the hearts of the public have grown the most weary. It is speeches like these that have become famous.

## LIVING WORDS FROM A DYING MAN
During the Napster days (think Spotify, but illegal), I scoured their database for every famous speech I could find.

35

I had entire libraries on my desktop filled with nothing but speeches from Martin Luther King Jr., Winston Churchill, Lou Holtz, and William Wallace (as voiced by Mel Gibson in *Braveheart*). However, my favorite speech of all time—the one that sends chills down my spine no matter how many times I listen to it—is the one Jimmy Valvano gave when he won the 1993 inaugural Arthur Ashe Courage and Humanitarian Award at the first ever ESPY Awards.

"Jimmy V," as he was called, was one of the most celebrated and beloved coaches in all of college basketball. He was passionate, vibrant, and animated—everything a ball coach should be. Jimmy V coached at Bucknell and Iona, but he is best known for his career at North Carolina State, where he led the Wolfpack to a last-second victory over Houston to win the NCAA championship in 1983. After capturing the title, the fiery coach sprinted aimlessly around the court in complete shock, arms flailing, looking for someone to hug. A decade later he had to be helped onstage to receive his award.

As the star-studded crowd stood to their feet in applause, Jimmy V quivered on aching feet, poised with a palpable sense of urgency behind the podium. You see, Jimmy V had a month to live. Maybe two. Three if he was lucky. Bone cancer had eaten him from the inside out, leaving him so weak he could barely stand. I could feel the gravity of the moment through the television. What this dying man was about to say was going to matter. The crowd knew it and I, as a mere fifteen-year-old, knew it as well.

Over the course of roughly 1,700 words, Jimmy V spoke without notes, not so much from the heart as from the aorta. It was as if Jimmy V, flowing with passion and intensity, had written his acceptance speech in his own blood. The network tried to hurry him up to get to commercial, but Jimmy V blew right past his time limit without an ounce of hesitation. *Now* was his time. *Now* was his moment. And everyone, including the network, knew it. For almost ten minutes he spoke not a word about the championships he had won in the past, the pain he felt in his body, or his fear of death. Instead, Jimmy V spoke about life and how to live it. "To me," he said, "there are three things we all should do every day."

> Number one is laugh. You should laugh every day.
> Number two is think. You should spend some time
> in thought. Number three is you should have your
> emotions moved to tears, could be happiness or joy.
> But think about it. If you laugh, you think and you
> cry, that's a full day. That's a heck of a day.[1]

I'll never forget those words. The cameras continued to roll as Jimmy V talked about his wife, Pam, and his three daughters, and the joy they had brought him throughout his life. He spoke about the importance of keeping your dreams alive even when all else fails. By the end of the speech, the entire crowd stood mesmerized, on the tips of their toes, in childlike amazement at the life found within this dying man.

More than anything, Jimmy V wanted his friends and

family to experience life and cherish it for the wonderful mystery that it is. "Don't give up," he said. "Don't ever give up."

Jesus once gave a similar speech. Except Jesus had only a few hours to live, not a few months. Betrayal, torture, and death by crucifixion awaited Jesus before the setting of the new sun. Weighted with a crushing sense of urgency and compassion, Jesus gathered his closest friends around the Passover table in order to say his final good-bye. Everything he had done, everything he had said, and everything he had established was about to be handed over to a group of ragtag fishermen and greedy tax collectors. Jesus' final words to his disciples are recorded in John 13–16 and have come to be known as his "Farewell Discourse."

Throughout these chapters, Jesus lays bare his heart in order to explain to his disciples the "full extent of his love."[2] In doing so, Jesus presents his disciples with an impossible command (John 13), encourages them with an inconceivable promise (John 14), and concludes with an intimate prayer for his friends (John 17). None of them could have predicted the *type* of love they were being invited into, and *how* close Jesus promised to be to them after his death. While "close and personal" described their relationship with Jesus up to this point, they were about to learn (and know from experience) an entirely new way of understanding their relationship to Christ.

## JOHN 13: AN IMPOSSIBLE COMMAND

In John 13, Jesus began his farewell to his friends. He didn't refer back to Israel's past to celebrate the mighty acts of God, typical of the Passover celebration. Instead, Jesus' words grabbed his disciples by the face and turned their attention squarely toward the future of a new community that would be guided by a "new" commandment. More than anything, Jesus wanted his friends to experience the depths of his love for them, and he also wanted to clearly reveal how they were to love one another (and God) in light of his impending death.

After serving the Passover meal, Jesus wrapped a towel around his waist, poured a basin of water, and washed his disciples' feet. In Jesus' day, due to the arid climate, the dusty roads, and the footwear (most of the people in the first century wore sandals), it was customary for a household or a host to provide a servant to wash the feet of guests before a meal. What *wasn't* customary was for a teacher to wash the feet of his disciples. To do so would be considered humiliating for the teacher and embarrassing for his followers. "Do you understand what I have done to you?" Jesus asked his disciples after washing their feet. "I have given you an example, that you also should do just as I have done to you" (John 13:12, 15). Often this is interpreted as a matter of humility and servanthood, but it was more than that: It was an expression of the type of love Jesus had for the disciples, a physical example of the new kind of love in which they were to love one another.

> A new commandment I give to you, that you love one
> another: *just as I have loved you*, you also are to love
> one another. By this all people will know that you are
> my disciples, if you have love for one another.
>
> JOHN 13:34-35, EMPHASIS ADDED

The fascinating part about this new command is not the first part. The disciples knew they were to love one another. The jaw-dropping addition was the revelation that they were to love one another *just as* Jesus loved them. What type (or kind) of love was Jesus referring to? He told them in John 15:9: "As the Father has loved me, so have I loved you."

What? Wait. How would the disciples possibly love one another with the *same love* in which the Father has eternally loved Jesus, the eternal Son? That's impossible! No wonder John 14 begins with the words, "Do not let your hearts be troubled" (John 14:1, NIV). Unless God performed some type of miracle, they would spend the rest of their lives striving and miserably failing at the last thing their Lord commanded them to do! How could they possibly love one another *just as* the Father loved his one and *only* Son?

## JOHN 14: AN INCONCEIVABLE PROMISE

Jesus didn't delay in providing the answer. Time was too short, and the disciples' hearts had grown far too weary. They needed to know how they were to fulfill the new command of Jesus, and they needed to know *now*. And *now* was the time. Jesus promised:

> If you love me, you will keep my commandments.
> And I will ask the Father, and he will give you
> another Helper, to be with you forever, even the
> Spirit of truth, whom the world cannot receive,
> because it neither sees him nor knows him. You

know him, for he dwells with you and will be in
you.

I will not leave you as orphans; I will come to you.
Yet a little while and the world will see me no more,
but you will see me. Because I live, you also will live.
In that day you will know that I am in my Father, and
you in me, and I in you. . . . And he who loves me
will be loved by my Father, and I will love him and
manifest myself to him. . . . If anyone loves me, he
will keep my word, and my Father will love him, and
we will come to him and make our home with him.

JOHN 14:15-23

Upon the heels of Jesus' impossible command came the *first*
of two inconceivable (and mysterious) promises of Jesus in
John's Gospel. Here, Jesus promised that his disciples *would*
be able to keep his commandments—including not only the
entire law of Moses but also the new command to love one
another with the very same love in which the Father has
eternally loved the Son. How could this be? How would this
happen? It would happen when the Father sent the disciples
"another Helper" to be "in" them—a Helper whom Jesus
defined as the "Spirit of truth."

In the Old Testament, it was the Holy Spirit who filled
prophets, priests, and kings to fulfill God's will. It was also
the Holy Spirit who filled the Tabernacle and Temple with
the glory of God's presence. But now, according to Jesus, the
*exact same* Holy Spirit would dwell in the disciples, allowing

them to personally share in the love between the Father and the Son! They would *know* this love because the Holy Spirit, as the eternal breath between the Father and the Son, would unite them with the one true Son—Jesus Christ.

Donald Fairbairn, professor of early Christianity at Gordon-Conwell Theological Seminary, affirms this mind-blowing reality in his commentary on this passage:

> The Spirit's dwelling within believers is the key that
> enables us to *know* that the Son is in the Father,
> that believers are in the Son and that the Son is in
> believers. The *mutual sharing* of relationship between
> Father and Son and between Son and believers
> depends on the Holy Spirit. The Spirit is the one
> who links us to that relationship by *uniting* us to the
> Son.[3]

In other words, the Holy Spirit would unite the disciples *by grace* to what Jesus knew *by nature*—the perfect love of the Father.[4] As we said in the last chapter, Jesus is the one and *only* begotten Son of God. He is the only one who has eternally known and enjoyed the familial love of the Father.[5] In order to know and participate in the fullness of this love, the disciples would have to be united (by the Holy Spirit) to the only begotten Son of God—the person of Jesus Christ. There is no other option. There is no plan B. There is no other way the disciples could fulfill *any* command of God outside of or independent of being united to the person of Jesus

Christ. *Only* Jesus Christ fulfilled every command given by the Father (see John 17:4). In this way, it was (and continues to be) God's eternal plan to sum up all things in Christ (see Ephesians 1:9-10).

At a time when things were the most uncertain, and the disciples' hearts the most troubled, they were to look forward to the day when the Holy Spirit would unite them in a mysterious (yet real) way to the resurrected Son of God, Jesus Christ. In this way (and this way alone), they would fulfill the new command to love one another with the very same love between the Father and the Son *in* Christ—united to him by grace. No wonder John would go on to later proclaim, "See what kind of love the Father has given to us, that we should be called children of God" (1 John 3:1). And children of God the disciples were to become, though not children by "divine status" or some kind of impersonal declaration from afar. No. The Father's love does not operate from a distance. It's not good enough for fathers to be close to their children—they want to be closer than close; they want to be "in" them. The late Brennan Manning once said, "Love by its nature seeks union."[6] And the disciples would be beloved children of God by virtue of their being united to the object of the Father's eternal love and affection—Jesus Christ himself.

United to Christ, sharing in the very same love between the Father and the Son, the disciples would finally *know* the fullness of the Father's love, because they would participate in it *themselves*. And I can tell you, as a father myself, there is no greater joy than when you tell your children you love them, and instead of hearing, "I love you too," you hear, "I know." It's a game changer; it's what all loving parents want for their children—for them to *know* the full extent of their love. Why? Because love fully received is the consummation of love given. And the mystery of the Father's eternal plan *has always* been to share the fullness of his love with those united to his one true Son, Jesus Christ.

It's one thing to speak of the disciples' union with Christ. But the mystery of God's eternal plan to unite all things *in* Christ will take a *second* unexpected turn—expanding not only to the disciples but to you and me.

## JOHN 17: AN INTIMATE PRAYER

It's no surprise that John 17 contains Jesus' longest recorded prayer. With death marching his way, carrying torches and weapons, Jesus lifted his eyes to heaven and cried out to his Abba. In what has been called "the High Priestly Prayer," Jesus pleaded with the Father that everything he had just revealed to his disciples would come to fruition. In doing this, Jesus wasn't doubting God's faithfulness. Instead, his prayer showed how *deeply* Jesus longed for his disciples to know from personal experience the joy of sharing in his Father's love. It was this love that sustained Jesus in life and death; it would be this very same love that would sustain his friends in life and death as well.

But surprisingly, the mystery of the disciples' union with Christ turns out not to be for them alone! For the mystery hidden within God from all eternity has been to bring *everyone* who believes in Christ into a perfect union (or "one-ness") with him! In this way, God would not be the God of only one nation or race of people, but Father to a brand-new humanity *in* Christ who would reveal his love to the world. Jesus prayed boldly:

> I do not ask for these [the disciples] only, but also for *those who will believe in me through their word*, that they may *all be one, just as* you, Father, are in me, and I in you, that *they also may be in us*, so that the world may believe that you have sent me. The glory that you have given me I have given to them, that they may be *one* even as we are *one, I in them and you in me*, that they may become *perfectly one*, so that the world may know that you sent me and loved them even as you loved me. . . . I made known to them your name, and I will continue to make it known, *that the love with which you have loved me may be in them, and I in them.*
>
> JOHN 17:20-23, 26, EMPHASIS ADDED

This prayer was a perfect summation of everything Jesus outlined in John 13–16, except that Jesus expanded the promise to include all those who would believe in him through the witness and words of his disciples. How would this happen? By the disciples abiding in their union with Christ and extending the *natural fruit* of the Father's love for the Son to one another (see John 15). "By this," Jesus said in

John 13:35, "all people will know that you are my disciples." In other words, through the disciples loving one another just as the Father loved the Son, the world would see and believe that Jesus *really was* sent of God and that God really does love the world *as much as* his only begotten Son. United to Christ, all those who believe would know *from personal experience* the love between the Father and the Son. Why? Because they too would be made "one" with the one true Son—Jesus Christ. "At this point," in the exuberant words of Robert Letham, "the whole universe should stop for half an hour in utter amazement and wonder. What more can we possibly say?"[7]

But there is more! Jesus' plea for all believers to be "one" is tethered to an equally amazing and wonderful promise! Listen to this: ". . . that they [all those who believe in Christ] may become perfectly one, *so that the world may know* that you sent me and loved them even as you loved me" (John 17:23, emphasis added). How would the world know that Jesus was sent of God and that God loves the world as much as he loved his own Son? It would not come through believers being united in doctrine or on social issues, but through loving one another just as the Father loved the Son. United to Christ by the Holy Spirit, believers would make known the love of the Father to the world! As we will see in the final chapter, it is *this* type of church and *this* type of love that the gates of hell cannot (and will never) overcome. And it is this type of church that will *continue* to change the world.

## A DEFINING MOMENT

Union with Christ, according to the apostle Paul, is not just a mystery but a profound mystery (see Ephesians 5:32). That being said, I'd like to provide a working definition for "union with Christ." From here on, when I use the phrase, I intend this meaning:

> The mysterious (yet real) joining of believers to the person of Jesus through the Spirit, thereby allowing them to share in the very same love between the Father and Son, and by extension, the Holy Spirit.

Or to say it more simply, union with Christ *brings believers into the life and love of the Trinity.*

Union with Christ does not mean, however, becoming divine ourselves. We don't become the fourth person of the Trinity when we are united to Christ. Nor do we become a son (or daughter) of God in the *exact same way* that Jesus is God's Son. As creatures created in the image of God, we are able, *by grace*, to share in the natural communion of love that has forever existed between the Father and the Son. This is afforded to you and to me as we are united to Christ through the eternal breath, who is the Holy Spirit.

As we love one another with this *type* of love, the world will see (and experience) God's presence on earth as it is (and always has been) in heaven. But you and I aren't just a part of the divine mystery of God; we also are a part of the story of God—a story filled with good and evil, joy and pain, life and death.

## THE STORY OF GOD

It's no mystery that the world we live in today is not as it should be, because the world, as you and I know it, is not as God *intended* it to be. And neither are we. Our hearts groan alongside all of creation with the pains of disunion. Hurt, strife, and discord seem to permeate the four corners of the earth, as well as the inner contours of our being.

Why doesn't the world reflect the love between the Father, Son, and Spirit? What happened that caused so much disunion in our hearts and within the world? And why is there such an intense longing in us for wholeness, peace, and oneness? Where does this longing come from? Why do we have it? And more importantly, will there ever be a time, in this life or the next, when God will perfectly fulfill our longing to be one with him and those around us?

In answering these questions, many point to the overarching story of God—Creation, Fall, redemption, and consummation (or new creation). While this framework is certainly helpful, I'd like to reframe the story of God in light of our focus on union. For the story of God is just as much (if not more so) a story of union, disunion, reunion, and the promise of perfect union. The concepts of union and oneness permeate Scripture from Genesis to Revelation. From the three-in-one God who existed "in the beginning" to the New Jerusalem coming down from heaven like a bride dressed for her husband at the end of history, the concept of union is one of the most clear and consistent themes in all of Scripture. In order to help us reframe the story of God (and our involvement in it), the next two chapters will be devoted to recasting the amazing story of God through the lens of union to disunion, and reunion to perfect union. Or, in the spirit of Jimmy V, "where we started, where we are, and where we're going to be."

## DISCUSSION QUESTIONS

1. *In the last discussion question of the previous chapter, the author asked if you thought it was possible for humans to share in the divine love between the Father and the Son. After reading this chapter, how might you answer that question now?*

2. *How does the thought of being united to the resurrected, living person of Jesus Christ change the way you view your relationship with him? How does it impact the way you view yourself?*

3. *When you picture yourself united to Christ, what images come to mind?*

4. *How does being "one" with Christ make you feel? Explain.*

# 5

# UNION TO DISUNION: WHO WE WERE AND WHAT WE LOST

*I think I heard a good man say*
*"God is love and love has made us."*
*But have you seen the news today?*
*I have and I think God is gone away.*

NOAH GUNDERSEN,
"EMPTY FROM THE START"

I USED TO WATCH *Dancing with the Stars* when it first came out. (I haven't watched one episode in several years. No real reason. I just lost interest.) What fascinated me about the show was how ordinary people learned to perform dances such as the cha-cha and the waltz in such a short amount of time. Granted, some contestants were horrific dancers—stiff, wooden, always bumping into their partner and stepping on their toes (cough . . . Jerry Springer . . . cough). Others, however, seemed to glide, twist, and circle effortlessly across the floor with their partner in tow. And when two professional dancers would pair up for a demonstration, it was as if they shared the same feet, legs, waist, and arms. Every part of their bodies moved and made room for the other at exactly the right time.

Oxford professor and theologian C. S. Lewis once described the relational union between the Father, Son, and Spirit as a kind of "dance" where all three persons of the Trinity make room for the others in a perpetual circle of self-giving and self-receiving love.[1] The Greek fathers of the church referred to this loving unity within the Trinity by using the fascinating (and baffling) term *perichoresis*. It is the *perichoresis* of the Father, Son, and Spirit that serves as the first of three specific unions found at the beginning of the Genesis story: the union of God, God's union with Adam, and Adam's union with Eve.

## UNION IN THE BEGINNING (PREHISTORY TO GENESIS 2)

*The union of God.* As we said, the early church employed the term *perichoresis* to describe the perfect union of life and love found within the Trinity.[2] Taken from the Greek words *peri* ("around") and *chorein* ("to give" or "to make room"), *perichoresis* describes the Greek fathers' understanding of the Trinity to be eternally "present with one another, for one another, and in one another."[3] Now, if you are like me, the "with one another" and "for one another" part of this description make complete sense. The fascinating (and baffling) parts surrounds the mysterious "in-ness" of God, or what some theologians call the "mutual indwelling" of the Father, Son, and Spirit. While I appreciate Lewis's dancing analogy, *perichoresis* has a much more graphic and physical connotation—one of mutual "interpenetration." Instead of simply dancing around one another, the Father, Son, and Spirit each, in the words of Gerald Bray, occupy the "same divine 'space.'"[4] Understood this way, *perichoresis* helps capture the divine "community of being" within the Trinity, where each person fills (or penetrates) one another while at the *same time* being perfectly filled (or penetrated) by the others as one God.

What I like about *perichoresis* is that it gives us a picture of the perfect union of life and love found within the Holy Trinity. And it is from this unity of persons that we see God the Father, Son, and Spirit giving themselves not only to one another but to the world. For it was God's divine intention and delight to give the fullness of his being both to creation and to the crowning work of creation: man and woman.

*God's union with Adam.* If I could personally witness any moment in Scripture, I would certainly choose Genesis 2:7. After creating the heavens and the earth, the Scriptures say that God "formed the man of dust from the ground." How remarkable it would have been to witness God fashioning Adam from nothing but dust! How the Father must have celebrated the completion of the Word spoken in Genesis 1:26: "Let us make man in our image, after our likeness." Out of everything God had made, Adam was specifically created to image the infinite life of God. This is what separated Adam from any other created thing.

But not only was Adam designed to be an *image bearer* of the triune God, Adam was created as an *embodied agent* uniquely designed to be filled with and participate in the loving community and intimate communion shared between the Father, Son, and Holy Spirit. We see *God the Father* graciously giving Adam a physical body through the declaration of the *Eternal Word* so that Adam might share in the loving relationship between the Father and the Son through the *Holy Spirit.* In this way, according to Dom Eugene Boylan, Adam was "destined to share—in a finite way, of course—in the life of the Blessed Trinity."[5] It was for this that Adam was created. It was this that separated the man from the plants, the animals, and even the angels themselves. And it would be the Holy Spirit, as the gift of bonding love between the Father and the Son,[6] who would unite Adam to the eternal life and love of the Trinity. "For the way the Father makes known his love," says Michael Reeves, "is precisely through giving his Spirit."[7]

But that time had not come upon Adam yet. For the Holy Spirit had not yet been breathed into the dust of the man. It's not until the second part of Genesis 2:7 that we read, "And [God] breathed into his [Adam's] nostrils the breath of life, and the man became a living creature." How I wish I could have been there! God breathed his *ruach* (Hebrew for "breath" or "spirit") into the man, not simply waking Adam to life but filling him with *Life himself*—the person of the Holy Spirit.[8]

God, by virtue of his nature, will not give anything less than the fullness of himself. As the Father, Son, and Spirit have eternally given themselves fully to one another, so the Holy Spirit gives Adam the fullness of his life and love. In doing so, the Holy Spirit breathes into (and brings Adam into) the loving communion (i.e., *perichoresis*) of the Father, Son, and Spirit. Now that is closer than close!

But God had something else in store for Adam—*someone* who would come from the body of the man in order to become "one flesh" with him. Her name was Eve.

*Adam's union with Eve.* After Adam became a "living creature," God brought all the animals before him to see what he would name them. But the text says there was "not found a helper fit for him" (Genesis 2:20). In other words, Adam himself did not have an equal. And according to God, this was "not good"; the man was considered to be "alone."

Therefore, God closed the eyes of the man and split his one person into two. God took a rib from the *ish* (Hebrew for "man") and fashioned the rib into an *ishshah* (Hebrew for "woman"). Here again I wonder what joy and delight God must have felt in fashioning the body of the woman. How the Father, Son, and Spirit must have marveled at the wonder and the beauty of that which would be called "woman."

After personally fashioning the woman, God presented man and woman to one another as the completion of themselves. Adam, seeing the woman for the first time, burst out in song:

> This at last is bone of my bones
>     and flesh of my flesh;
> she shall be called Woman,
>     because she was taken out of Man.

GENESIS 2:23

Instead of leaving Eve "out of Man," God united the *ish* and *ishshah* together as "one." In this first picture of a marriage, God declared of the man and the woman, "Therefore a man shall leave his father and his mother and hold fast to his wife, and they shall become one flesh" (Genesis 2:24). This one-flesh union was perfect, even though it neither compromised nor diminished the man or the woman as individual persons. They were two, yet one, enjoying a singular plurality with one other.[9] By virtue of Eve's union with Adam, she, too, shared in the communion of love between the Father, Son, and Holy Spirit; as "one flesh" with Adam, how could she not? Everything that belonged to Adam now belonged to Eve by virtue of her union with him. God declared the woman to be Adam's "wife" (verses 24-25).

The union that Adam and Eve shared with God (and one another) would serve as a prototype for the rest of humanity. All of their descendants would, like them, be united to the life and love of the Father, Son, and Holy Spirit. And according to Genesis 1:31, God looked upon all that the Word spoke into existence and declared it to be "very good." And so it was, for a time.

## DISUNION ON EARTH (GENESIS 3–11)

Sometime after God joined Adam and Eve to himself and one another, a serpent entered the story. According to Genesis 3:1, the serpent was "more crafty than any other beast of the field." It's not until Revelation 12:9 that the serpent is identified as being "the devil and Satan." According to the book of Ezekiel, sometime before the creation of Adam and Eve, Satan was an "anointed guardian cherub" who rebelled against God due to his pride, violence, and narcissism. He was cast to the ground because of his unrighteousness, and his venomous nature was "exposed . . . before kings" (Ezekiel 28:1-17). Adam and Eve likely had prior knowledge of the serpent and might have even dealt with him before his appearance in Genesis 3:1. In any case, the serpent was a part of creation, and therefore was under the authority of Adam and Eve as God's representatives.

Dripping with indignation and jealous pride, Satan approached Adam and Eve. His intent? A coup d'état. Knowing God's command to the man (and by extension the woman) that "of the tree of the knowledge of good and evil you shall not eat" (Genesis 2:17), and having himself failed to overthrow God's rule and authority, Satan attempted to usurp it by convincing Adam and Eve to enter into solidarity with *him* instead of with God—in other words, to commit spiritual adultery. To have Adam and Eve enter into an unholy union with Satan would thereby establish him as the "god of this world" (2 Corinthians 4:4). But entering into such a union would require a covenant meal.

Enticed by the tree, and having considered Satan's offer to "be like God" (Genesis 3:5), Adam and Eve in one accord willingly consumed the fruit. In reaching up, picking, and consciously biting, chewing, and internalizing the meal, the man and woman broke their union with God and abdicated their authority and power to Satan. In the haunting words of Meredith Kline:

> By eating the forbidden fruit and accepting Satan's explanation of the world over God's, Adam and Eve sinned and in doing so switched their allegiance from God over to Satan. Their eating of the fruit was the solemn ceremony of the covenantal relationship they had just entered into with Satan.[10]

Rather than abiding in the love they already shared with God, Adam and Eve exchanged their union with God for that which they considered to be better, more pleasurable. They lustfully traded in the love of God for a lie, thereby breaking their union with God. Instead of being one with the life and love of the Trinity, Adam and Eve found themselves *separated* from God—estranged from the eternal life of the Father, Son, and Holy Spirit. Divorced from Life himself, Adam and Eve "died," just as God said they would.

But Adam and Eve didn't just keel over dead after eating the fruit. So, what happened? Although physical death would eventually render Adam and Eve back to dust, thus reversing the created order, the immediate death Adam and Eve suffered was their own spiritual death—a death the Bible describes as alienation from God's Spirit (see Colossians 1:21). When Adam and Eve ate the fruit of the forbidden tree, they "expired" spiritually: They "breathed out" the Spirit of God who united them to the love of the Father and the Son. The divorcing of the Spirit from the body is the very definition of death itself.

Divorced from God and dead to his Spirit, Adam and Eve also experienced disunion and death in relation to one another. This is evidenced not only by their bickering and finger-pointing over their sin (Genesis 3:12-13) but also in God's subsequent addressing of them as individual entities *rather than* as a unified whole (Genesis 3:16-19). In choosing to unite themselves with Satan, Adam and Eve found that every aspect of their lives and every aspect of the creation they had been given became distorted from the way God designed it. Instead of their being a blessing to the earth, all of creation was now cursed because of them. Instead of their being fruitful and multiplying, the fruit of their union with Satan produced pain, suffering, and physical death. Where perfect order and union once reigned through Adam and Eve, utter disorder and disunion now reigned.

## DISUNION DISTRIBUTED
## (GENESIS 12—MALACHI)

After Genesis 3, disunion not only reigned, it consumed people. Because Adam and Ever were separated from God's Spirit, physical and spiritual death passed on to all of their descendants. Every person born from the union of the man and the woman would be conceived in the same state Adam and Eve found themselves after the Fall.[11] And the body, devoid of the Spirit, who is Life, equals death.

From Genesis 3 to Malachi, disunion, discord, and death

become the prevalent theme, as murder, rape, adultery, and injustice plague the entire human race. But God, in his faithfulness, sends his people prophets, priests, and kings to comfort and reassure them of his steadfast love and mercy. And while disunion spreads across the whole earth, God continues to chase after that which he lost at the Fall—union with his bride.

Throughout the Old Testament, God consistently refers to himself as a "husband" and his covenant people as his "wife" or "bride."[12] Although humans divorced themselves from God, God remained faithful, committed to the union they once shared. In order to illustrate the extent of his faithfulness, God called a man by the name of Hosea to marry a well-known prostitute who, shortly after her marital union with Hosea, returned to her adulterous ways. Grief-stricken, Hosea was given the command of God to pursue his wayward bride as a picture of God's *own* pursuit of his adulterous people. It is through Hosea that God makes a beautiful promise to his people (and us):

> In that day, declares the LORD, you will call me
> "My Husband," and no longer will you call me "My
> Baal." For I will remove the names of the Baals from
> her mouth, and they shall be remembered by name
> no more. And I will make for them a covenant on
> that day with the beasts of the field, the birds of the
> heavens, and the creeping things of the ground. And
> I will abolish the bow, the sword, and war from the

land, and I will make you lie down in safety. *And I will betroth you to me forever.* I will betroth you to me in righteousness and in justice, in steadfast love and in mercy. I will betroth you to me in faithfulness. And you shall know the LORD.

HOSEA 2:16-20, EMPHASIS ADDED

The perfect union God once shared with his people will one day be fully restored. But how? When? How could such a divine love be united once again with sinful humanity? How would God cross the infinite abyss separating himself and his wayward bride?

The answer would come in the most unlikely of ways, and through another "fruit" of sorts—not the fruit of a tree but the fruit of a young Jewish girl—fruit that humanity would not reach up to acquire but that would come down to humanity: wrapped in swaddling clothes, enfleshed in warm skin, lying in a manger.

## DISCUSSION QUESTIONS

1. *How have you understood the Trinity of God the Father, Son, and Spirit in the past? What is your current understanding?*

2. *Did this chapter clarify or complicate your understanding of the Trinity? Explain.*

3. *Read Genesis 2:7. The author suggests that God breathed his Holy Spirit into Adam, filling Adam with (and bringing Adam into) the life and love of the*

*Trinity. Is this interpretation different from what you have previously believed? Explain.*

4. *The "Fall," as recorded in Genesis 3:1-6, is sometimes presented as Satan tricking a gullible Adam and Eve into sinning against God. How do you view the motivation behind Adam and Eve's sin differently after reading this chapter? Did this chapter change your view of sin? If so, explain.*

5. *God is described throughout the Old Testament as a "husband." How does this title differ from your current understanding of God?*

# 6

## REUNION TO PERFECT UNION: WHO WE ARE AND WHAT WE WILL BE

*Thou hast mingled, O LORD, Thy divinity with our humanity,*
*and our humanity with Thy divinity, Thy life with our*
*mortality, and our mortality with Thy life; Thou hast received*
*that which is ours, and given us that which is Thine, to the*
*life and salvation of our souls: glory be to Thee forever.*

ANCIENT LITURGY OF ST. JAMES

ANGELS ON HIGH. Stars from above. Heavenly peace. When I think about the Son of God becoming human, these are the images that come to mind. However, the night Jesus Christ was born was much more earthy—the night when infinity dwindled to infancy.

### REUNION: INFINITY DWINDLED TO INFANCY (MATTHEW 1—REVELATION 20)

Beloved poet Gerard Manley Hopkins captures the earthiness that surrounded that holy night in Bethlehem.

*Of her who not only*
*Gave God's infinity*

*Dwindled to infancy*
*Welcome in womb and breast,*
*Birth, milk, and all the rest*
*But mothers each new grace*
*That does now reach our race.*[1]

The "becoming flesh" of the eternal Son of God not only included angelic voices in the heavenlies and bright shining stars. It involved a woman's womb, an umbilical cord, blood, water, milk, and breasts. It disturbs every religious fiber in my body to think that the Eternal Word who existed with God in the beginning somehow became a solid ball of cells that developed into a human embryo within the womb of a teenage girl. The picture is too messy, too down-to-earth, and far too human for my evangelical sensibilities. When I think of the Incarnation in this way, I hear a little voice in my head shouting, *God is God and we are not!* I picture a line in the sand, with the word *divinity* written on one side and *humanity* on the other. I hear Gandalf shout, "You shall not pass!"

Yet the scandal of the Incarnation is that God the Son, the second person of the Trinity, stepped over the line that separated his divinity from our humanity. In doing so he bridged (more like united) both full divinity and absolute humanity within his own person. In this way, the incarnation of the Eternal Word, who existed with God in the beginning and is God, screams (in a raspy Middle Eastern voice), "God is God and I am he! Touch me. Hear me. Smell me. Believe in me."

I like angels on high and stars from above a little better. Those images are more comfortable. More safe.

—

The incarnation of the Son of God is the opposite of safe. It's daring, bold, and in-your-face. It transcends human logic and stretches our understanding of both the nature of divinity and the capacity of humanity. How can divinity be fully human? How can a human be fully divine? And more precisely, how can a person be both fully human and fully divine at the *exact* same time?

These were the questions the early church fathers wrestled with. For them (as well as for most of us today) it was easier to maintain that the person of Jesus, as God's Son, was fully divine. It was quite another to believe that Jesus, as a person, was fully human. And it was almost heretical to believe full divinity and full humanity could be perfectly united within a single person!

Therefore, it will be helpful for us to consider how the early church understood the relation between the two natures of Jesus as well as the importance of the Incarnation for salvation. But be forewarned. The early church fathers wrestled deeply with the flesh. Deeply. I'll allow them to explain.

## WRESTLING WITH THE FLESH

Trying to maintain the full "humanness" of Jesus in light of his full divinity in the first few hundred years of the church was like trying to keep a beach ball under water. It was the main topic of the first several early church councils, as the early church fathers labored tirelessly to maintain the church's unity around a unified Christ. Like today, some of the fathers found it problematic (and theologically suspect) for full divinity and full humanity to be perfectly "one" within a human being. One such person was a guy named Nestorius, the influential bishop of Constantinople.

Nestorius believed that Christ was fully human and fully divine; he had no problem with that. But what Nestorius couldn't reconcile was how God the Word was united (made one) with the person of Jesus. Such a union of divinity and humanity seemed to blur the Creator-creature distinction. Nestorius posited God the Word to be a *separate* person from the man Jesus and that the Word (as a separate person) only indwelt Jesus, making Jesus merely an embodied agent of divinity, but not the divine Word himself.[2]

This did not sit well with many of the church fathers, especially with one named Cyril of Alexandria. Cyril wrote several letters to Nestorius vehemently opposing his dividing Christ in half. According to Cyril, Christ had to be God the Word incarnate, not just a man indwelt by God the Word. If not, then humanity as a whole would still be separated from God and dead in their sin.

*Wait. What?* Isn't salvation through faith in Christ alone? Yes, it is. But for salvation to be possible by faith, Jesus had to unite the fullness of humanity with the fullness of divinity within his own person. Let me explain.

In order for human sin to be forgiven, an *actual human* had to die. God's justice demanded this since it was humans who sinned and not God himself. And yet, only *one who was absolutely God* could atone for sin! Therefore, Christ *had* to serve as an atonement (at-*one*-ment) uniting divinity and humanity within his person. If not, then humanity's sin could not be divinely forgiven. For in the famous words of Gregory Nazianzen, "That which he [Christ] has not assumed he has not healed."[3] In Christ (literally, *in* the person of Christ) God united humanity and divinity together as *one* in order to fully heal the human condition and atone for humanity's sin.

In this way, Jesus not only serves as *an* atoning sacrifice for our sin on the cross, Jesus Christ *is* the at-*one*-ment— uniting humanity and divinity within himself so that, by faith, we may "become partakers of the divine nature, having escaped from the corruption that is in the world because of sinful desire" (2 Peter 1:4). This is precisely what the writer of Hebrews says:

> For this reason he [Christ] *had to be* made like them, *fully human in every way* [flesh and blood (verse 14)], in order that he might become a merciful and faithful high priest in service to God, and that he might make *atonement for the sins of the people.*
> HEBREWS 2:17, NIV, EMPHASIS ADDED

This passage (as well as the entire book of Hebrews) makes it clear that Christ, as the divine Son of God and second person of the Trinity, *had to* assume the fullness of human nature within his divine person in order to be a proper at-*one*-ment between God and humanity. If not, then all of humanity would still be separated from God, dead in their sin, and waiting to be united to God through some other divine person! Remember, the greatest tragedy of the Fall was not the introduction of sin, it was the *effect* that sin had on humanity—separation from God. So Jesus Christ, as the second Adam, reconciled sinful humanity *into* God's divinity by perfectly uniting both within his flesh-and-blood person.

Again, this is the *exact* point the writer of Hebrews makes in saying:

> Since the children [humanity] have *flesh and blood*,
> he [Christ] too *shared in their humanity* so that by
> his death he might break the power of him who
> holds the power of death—that is, the devil—and
> free those who all their lives were held in slavery by
> their fear of death.
>
> HEBREWS 2:14-15, NIV, EMPHASIS ADDED

So with salvation itself at stake, in AD 431 the church fathers called a church council to Ephesus (modern-day Turkey). Although the council itself was a bit of a mess, the end result was a clear condemnation of Nestorius's view. Cyril and others were able to hold together the (already fledgling) unity of the church by maintaining the unity of full divinity and full humanity within the one person of Jesus Christ.

## SEEING LIKE CYRIL

So how does viewing the Incarnation like Cyril help us understand God's union with humanity and our union with Christ today? Immensely. But let me point out three key things.[4]

First, Cyril shows us that *salvation (as a whole) is an indivisible union.* While some like to prioritize certain aspects of salvation and give weight to some parts of Christ's work over others, the response of Cyril and others to the Nestorian controversy teaches us the importance of the *entire* scope of God's redemptive work through Christ. For instance, in much contemporary preaching, the cross of Jesus Christ is said to be the "most central act" of God. While the Cross is certainly central, it is only *one part* of the entire scope of salvation. The early church fathers understood this in a deep way. For according to Cyril, if the Incarnation were misconstrued, so that Christ did not unite humanity and divinity in his person, then the Cross would be for nothing!

Does this mean that more weight should be placed on the Incarnation than on the Cross? By no means! If the fully divine and fully human Christ had not died on the cross, then our sins would not be forgiven and God's justice would be unmet. The same logic can be extended to the Resurrection, the Ascension, and the glorification and future return of Christ. The most central act of salvation, then, is not one of these but *all of these.* United together as "one" they constitute the most central act of God in human history.

Second, seeing the Incarnation like Cyril makes clear that *salvation is not "something," it's "someone."* For most of my life,

I considered salvation a "thing" that God bestowed upon me from afar. However, the church fathers understood that our sin was atoned for, not outside the physical person of Jesus Christ, but *within* his actual body. Therefore, Christ *himself* is salvation, justification, sanctification, and any other spiritual blessing.[5] If this were not true, then we would be at risk of "rending Christ asunder," as John Calvin famously said. To share in the salvation that is Christ, then, we must be joined (made "one") with the actual, living, incarnate, resurrected person of Jesus Christ. Again, John Calvin, writing in *Institutes of the Christian Religion*, affirms this: "For we await salvation from him [Christ] not because he appears to us afar off, but because he makes us, *ingrafted into his body*, participants not only in all his benefits but also in himself."[6]

Third, Cyril helps us see that *union with the person of Jesus Christ is possible and necessary for salvation*. Instead of believers simply having a "close relationship" with Jesus or "appearing" to be one with him, the Incarnation proves that humanity is capable of being *united* (made one) with divinity—and that divinity is capable of being (and willing to be) *united* to humanity. If not, the incarnation of the Son of God in the person of Jesus Christ could not have happened! Theologian Robert Letham states:

> The Trinity created us with a capacity to live in him [Christ], as creatures in and with our Creator. The incarnation proves it. If it were not so and could not be so, then Jesus Christ—God and man—could not

be one person, for the difference between Creator and creature would be so great that the incarnation would not be possible.[7]

But not only is union with Christ possible, it is also *necessary* for salvation. This is why Paul uses the phrase "*in* Christ" 164 times[8] throughout his thirteen letters to describe the *actual place* where salvation, justification, and eternal life are found. Salvation, according to Paul, is not just "because of Christ" or "on account of Christ," but literally *in* the living, breathing person of Jesus Christ himself.

When I think of salvation actually being *in* Christ, I can't help but think about a scene in the sitcom *Arrested Development*. In this fictional account of the ridiculously rich and highly dysfunctional Bluth family, the patriarch of the family, George Bluth Sr., is arrested for defrauding investors of the family's real estate business. He entrusts the financial welfare of the family to his son, Michael. Determined to prove his competence, Michael quickly revives the only reliable source of income the family has left: the Bluth Original Frozen Banana Stand.

Opened in 1953 by George Sr., the banana-shaped stand quickly became a popular "joint" for tasty treats (as well as the illegal buying and selling of marijuana). And no one knows the ins and outs of the banana stand like George Sr.

Michael works around the clock selling frozen bananas In hopes of turning a profit. But despite his best effort, the banana stand fails to be the financial savior Michael expects. Desperate, he visits his father in prison to seek his "expert" advice. But the only advice George Sr. will offer is the repeated (and somewhat patronizing) assurance that "there's always money in the banana stand."

After trying everything, Michael determines there is no money in the banana stand. Disgusted with himself, his father, and the stand itself, Michael sets the banana stand ablaze, burning it to the ground. He proudly admits his act of arson to his father.

> **George Sr.:** *You what???*
> **Michael:** Burned it right down to the ground.
> **George Sr.:** Are you crazy? There was money in that banana stand.
> **Michael:** Well, it's all gone now, Dad, and it was my decision.
> **George Sr.:** There was 250,000 dollars lining the walls of the banana stand!
> **Michael:** *What?*
> **George Sr.:** Cash, Michael.
> **Michael:** Why didn't you tell me that?
> **George Sr.:** How much clearer can I say, "There's always money in the banana stand"?

As Michael did with the money, how many times have we objectified Jesus, making him a *means* to our salvation instead of Salvation himself? We work, pray, and strive to acquire the benefits of Christ on the cross without ever stopping to realize that eternal life isn't something God produces, but someone God offers—Jesus Christ himself. I imagine if Cyril (or Paul, for that matter) were alive today, he might stand up in the middle of most contemporary sermons regarding the nature of salvation and shout, "How much clearer can I say, 'Salvation is *in* Christ'?"

While salvation in Christ is certainly a "profound mystery," there is coming a day when our union with him will be made visible, tangible, and perfect. It is toward that day we hope, pray, and turn next.

## PERFECT UNION: HEAVEN ON EARTH (REVELATION 21–22)

One of my major handicaps in life is the fact that I am a perfectionist. Actually, I'm a bit obsessive. Okay, I'm *a lot* obsessive. Each of these "disorders" stems from the fact that in the fourth grade I was diagnosed with Tourette's syndrome.

For those who don't know, Tourette's syndrome (TS) is a neurological disorder that causes a person to "tic." Tics can be both vocal and motor in nature. Motor tics involve sudden, brief, and repetitive movements, while vocal tics involve things like uttering sounds and repeating random words and phrases (and yes, even swear words).[9] TS is also directly linked to obsessive-compulsive disorder (OCD) and attention-deficit hyperactivity disorder (ADHD), as well as to anxiety and depression—all of which I have suffered from over the years.[10] Needless to say, living with TS has made life difficult and, at the same time, a lot more humorous.

The other evening, as I was watching television, my six-year-old son, Cole (who has Tourette's as well), saw me "tic" from across the room. He asked, "Dad, will there be Tourette's in heaven?"

"Nope," I said confidently. "And you know what else?" I shot back, looking at Cole with wide-eyed wonder and lifted brows. "There will be a day when there will be no Tourette's on *earth*!"

Cole sat stunned. I could tell that his Sunday school theology had been blown out of the water. "One day," I continued, "God is going to make all things new here—right here on planet Earth." And with that, like any exhausted father, I sat back in my chair and changed the subject (and the channel), hoping the seed had been planted.

The ultimate hope and end of the Christian story is *not* heaven. While this may be surprising to hear, Revelation 21–22 makes it clear heaven will be established on earth—not just any earth, but a new, transformed, re-created earth. Listen to John's revelation of what is not the end but rather the new beginning:

> Then I saw a new heaven and a new earth, for the first heaven and the first earth had passed away, and the sea was no more. And I saw the holy city, new Jerusalem, coming down out of heaven from God, prepared as a bride adorned for her husband. And I heard a loud voice from the throne saying, "Behold, the dwelling place of God is with man. He will

dwell with them, and they will be his people, and God himself will be with them as their God. He will wipe away every tear from their eyes, and death shall be no more, neither shall there be mourning, nor crying, nor pain anymore, for the former things have passed away."

And he who was seated on the throne said, "Behold, I am making all things new." Also he said, "Write this down, for these words are trustworthy and true." And he said to me, "It is done! I am the Alpha and the Omega, the beginning and the end. To the thirsty I will give from the spring of the water of life without payment. The one who conquers will have this heritage, and I will be his God and he will be my son."

REVELATION 21:1-7

Since the beginning of creation, the world and its inhabitants have been the focal point of God's activity. Instead of God being a kind of divine clock maker who simply created the earth, set it spinning, and walked away, God has been directly and personally involved in every aspect of earth's history. And according to John, God will continue to do so throughout eternity future. Why? Because "the earth is the LORD's, and everything in it, the world, and all who live in it" (Psalm 24:1, NIV). Dutch theologian Abraham Kuyper is a bit more specific: "There is not a square inch in the whole domain of our human existence over which Christ, who is

Sovereign over *all*, does not cry, 'Mine!'"[11] Go ahead. Point your finger at something. It's God's. God owns every square inch of everything you see.

Not only has God focused his attention on earth because it's his, he does so because the earth is *good*. While there are certain theological beliefs that consider the earth to be bad and anticipate (and even celebrate) the complete and utter destruction of the planet, this is *not* representative of John's revelation of a renewed heaven and a new earth in the passage above. Neither is it in line with what the Father has already declared over creation. After the Eternal Word created the heavens and the earth, the Father looked over all his Son had made and proclaimed it *tov meod*, or "very good"!

We naturally object to the "goodness" of the earth today. Disasters, hunger, sickness, and war seem to define the make-up of the world around us. But these things are exactly the point! Ever since Adam and Eve handed dominion of the world (and everything in it) over to Satan, the ancient serpent has pillaged and ravaged every square inch of it. It is *this* that isn't good. To the Father, every square inch of the earth itself is still very good.

*But how?* Imagine if a bully were to steal, trample, or otherwise make a mockery of a craft or painting one of my boys made for me at school. Would that make the creation itself bad? Would my son or the original intent of his creation be evil as a result? No. The marring of his creation would reveal the evil and unjust nature of the bully! In the same way, the Father's declaration over what his Son made in the beginning is the same declaration over all of creation today. God does not consider the earth to be evil or bad. No. Instead, he considers what Satan (and fallen humanity) has done to the earth to be evil and bad. In fact, he hates how Satan has twisted, mangled, and mocked his Son's creation. But the Father will get the last word in the end. Write it down. And his final word will be even better than the first.

According to John's revelation, when Jesus returns to earth a second time, he will bring with him a *new* heaven and a *new* earth. In doing so, God declares that he will make "all things new." And as a loving Father, how could he not?

Think back to the analogy of the bully ravaging the creation of one of my boys. What do you think I would do when my son returned home with his compromised creation in hand? Would I throw it away as damaged goods? Would I burn it in complete and utter disgust? No! I'd love his creation even more knowing his intent and grieve over the shame he must have felt in having his creation defiled. But not only that, I would *personally* work as long as needed and spend as much money as required to ensure that what my son had made was completely restored.

Knowing how bullies are, however, to only restore his creation back to its *original* state would allow the bully to still snicker over what he had done. Therefore, out of compassion and vindication for my son I would *renew* his creation in such a way that it would be light-years *better* than before. But I wouldn't stop there. In order to glorify my son and disgrace the bully, I would unexpectedly show up to school one day with my son, where we would unveil our new creation to all those who witnessed the injustice. We would parade our new work around for all to see. I might even throw a party for the entire school in celebration.

This is what God the Father intends to do. When Jesus ascended back to his Father in heaven, he promised that he and his Father would not only restore all of creation but immediately begin the work of re-creating the world into something brand-new. In this way, the end of the age will literally be a "homecoming" as God the Father will reestablish his eternal dwelling place on this new earth. There will be no death, mourning, crying, pain, or Tourette's!

## A NEW HUMANITY

Along with a renewed earth, humanity itself will be fully restored—transformed into something completely new and better. For in that day, we will be transformed into the image of the living, incarnate, resurrected, and now glorified person of Jesus Christ!

Christ is described in the New Testament as being the "first-born" (Colossians 1:15) and the "firstfruits" (1 Corinthians 15:23) of all creation. In this way, Christ is not only the first in time, but the first in type—indicative of the entire harvest to follow.[12] This means that all those united to Christ can be confident, according to the apostle Paul, "that He who began a good work in you will perfect it until the day of Christ Jesus" (Philippians 1:6, NASB).[13] *Perfect*. I like that word!

In this passage, "the day of Christ Jesus" refers to the future coming of Christ himself. And when the resurrected

Christ returns to earth, his "work" will finally be complete. What work is this? It's the entire scope of salvation!

Since the entire scope of humanity finds its fullest expression in the incarnate Christ,[14] whatever is true of Christ's divine person now (other than his unique divinity) is the present reality of all believers everywhere. Therefore, all those who are in Christ have *already participated* in Christ's life (Hebrews 3:14), baptism (Galatians 3:27), crucifixion (Galatians 2:20), death (Colossians 2:20), burial (Romans 6:4), resurrection (1 Corinthians 15:22), and glorification (Romans 8:17; Ephesians 2:6).[15] Since Jesus Christ, as the divine Son of God, united the fullness of our humanity in his person, when Christ was crucified on the cross, you and I (in our humanity) were crucified with him. When Christ died for our sin, we died with him to sin. When Christ was resurrected from the dead, we were resurrected with him to new life. When Christ was glorified, we too were glorified and now (present tense) are "seated . . . with him in the heavenly places" (Ephesians 2:6).

But while the entire scope of Christ's salvation has already been fully *inaugurated* in the lives of believers, the completion of the work has yet to be *consummated*. When Christ comes to perfect our union with him, we will be transformed into *his* likeness and into *his* image. Instead of being restored to the image of the first Adam, we will be transformed into the image of the perfect Image himself—the firstborn of the new creation to come, Jesus Christ. *Perfection*.

Until then, how does union with Christ affect the way we live in the here and now? What real difference does it make in the way we understand ourselves and the world around us? How does sharing in the love between the Father and the Son shape the way we view the spiritual disciplines and approach Christ's mission locally and globally? And more specifically, how does our reality in Christ impact our everyday lives— lives filled with both the extraordinary and the mundane? It is to these questions surrounding our divine reality *in Christ* that we turn our attention.

## DISCUSSION QUESTIONS

1. *When you think of humanity and divinity, the physical and the spiritual, do you see them as compatible or incompatible? Explain.*

2. *Nestorius believed that God the Son and Jesus the person were not one but two* different *people. He did not, however, believe that humanity and divinity were united ("made one") in the person of Jesus Christ. Can you sympathize with Nestorius not wanting to unite the two? Why was his view a threat to salvation?*

3. *When you think of eternal life, do you typically think of it as something God grants from a distance? Read John 11:25 and 14:6. How does Jesus speak of eternal life?*

4. *Does it give you hope to know that God has promised to perfectly transform you into the image of his Son here on a renewed earth? If so, explain.*

PART TWO

The Divine Reality

# 7

## PERSONAL IDENTITY:
## THE MOST LOVED

*To all who did receive him, who believed in his name, he gave
the right to become children of God, who were born, not of blood
nor of the will of the flesh nor of the will of man, but of God.*

JOHN 1:12-13

IN ONE OF MY FAVORITE MOVIES, *Throw Momma from the
Train*, Danny DeVito plays an emotionally stunted middle-
aged man named Owen. When Owen was a young child, his
father passed away, leaving him to be raised by his overbear-
ing and verbally abusive "momma," played by Anne Ramsey.
In a heartwarming scene, Owen convinces his friend Larry
(played by Billy Crystal) to view his beloved coin collection. Lying on the floor in front of a small wooden chest,
Owen pridefully presents his coins to his friend. "This one
is a nickel," Owen says gently. "And this one also is a nickel.
And here is a quarter. And another quarter. And a penny."
    Taken aback, Larry reminds Owen that "the purpose of a

coin collection is that the coins are worth something." Owen rasps, "Oh, but they are!"

> This one here, I got in change when my dad took me to see Peter, Paul, and Mary. And this one, I got in change when I bought a hot dog at the circus. . . . Ah, this one is my favorite. This is Martin and Lewis at the Hollywood Palladium. Look at that—see the way it shines, huh? The little eagle? I loved my dad a lot. . . . [All this is] change my daddy let me keep.

For Owen, what was special about each coin was not its rarity or uniqueness, but how it reminded him of his father and the loving relationship they shared. In many ways, the coins reminded Owen of *who he was*—a prized and beloved son of his father, with whom his dad was well pleased. That sense of identity gave Owen the strength to endure many of life's hardships, particularly the accusing and degrading voice of his momma (even though he eventually wanted to throw her off a train!).

As God's eternal Son, Jesus received everything that belonged to his Father (John 16:15). Jesus was given all authority in heaven and on earth (Matthew 28:18)—the authority to proclaim freedom to the captives and recovery of sight to the blind, and the authority to set free all the oppressed (Luke 4:18). Jesus also held a special anointing to proclaim the good news to the poor. These gifts (and many others) the Father freely gave to his Son through the Holy Spirit.

While each of these was vital to Jesus' life and ministry, none of them defined Jesus as a person. Jesus knew himself to be much more than gifted; he understood himself to be the beloved and pleasing Son of his Father. It was the reality of his Father's affirmation, love, and pleasure that Jesus cherished above any other.

In the Gospel of Matthew, we witness the moment when the Father publicly announces the reality and depth of his fatherly affection for his Son—an affection that defined Jesus in both life and death:

> As soon as Jesus was baptized, he went up out of the water. At that moment heaven was opened, and he saw the Spirit of God descending like a dove and. alighting on him. And a voice from heaven said, "This is my Son, whom I love; with him I am well pleased."
> MATTHEW 3:16-17, NIV

Jesus' baptism marked his entry into public ministry—a time that would be filled with great joy and tremendous suffering. It would have been understandable for the Father to commission Jesus by highlighting his unique divinity, his absolute authority, or his divine anointing. To be charged in such a way would have surely provided the comfort and confidence Jesus needed for the task ahead. But at this particularly vulnerable moment in Jesus' life, the Father mentions not a word concerning any of these. Instead, he chooses to affirm Jesus' personal identity as "my Son, whom I love; [with whom] I am well pleased."

This threefold affirmation from his Father defined Jesus at his core. While his authority and anointing were critical, it was the Father's affirmation of his being the beloved Son that gave Jesus the strength to set his face toward Jerusalem to endure the cross. It was his Father's pleasure and delight that sustained Jesus in the face of accusation, humiliation, and death. As the beloved Son of God, Jesus had nothing to prove, nothing to defend, and nothing to attain. He was free to live, love, and minister to the hurting, the sick, and the poor.

Jesus' strong sense of identity stands in stark contrast to the fragile identity many of us have today. We pride ourselves on being hardworking, independent, gifted, and competent. We root our identities in what college we went to, how much money we have, and what we have accomplished in life. When these go uncelebrated, unnoticed, or even challenged or lost, we fall into deep despair and begin questioning our self-worth, importance, and purpose in life. No wonder so much time and energy is spent on promoting our accomplishments, our successes, our visions, and our images on Facebook, Instagram, and Twitter. No wonder we find ourselves nervously protecting our brands, our reputations, our denominations, our political parties, our incomes, and our ministries. When our identities are tethered to externals, our sense of self-worth is always in danger. In the end, we become hypersensitive, insecure, and discontent, always comparing ourselves to the next parent, the next young professional, the next pastor across town.

But as believers united to Christ, our identities are not in what we do (or even in what Christ has done) but in *who Christ is*. And at the core of Jesus' identity is this deep, abiding, and freeing reality that he is the beloved Son in whom the Father is well pleased. In this chapter, we will look at our own reality, as adopted sons and daughters of God whom the Father loves and with whom he is likewise fully pleased.

## "THIS IS MY SON": EMBRACING OUR DIVINE ADOPTION

I suspect when many of us hear the word *adoption* we think of movies like *Annie, The Blind Side*, and *Despicable Me*, where orphaned children are graciously incorporated into a family. But while movies like these warm the heart, they tend to portray the faulty stigma that adoption is mostly a change in legal status: a child is considered to be a son or a daughter, but not *really*. This can be seen in *Annie* where she continues to be referred to as "little *orphan* Annie" well after being adopted by Daddy Warbucks. Speaking on behalf of many parents who have adopted a child, this should not be!

Unfortunately, many Christians today view divine adoption in much the same way. To be adopted by God is seen to be more or less a legal transfer of rights and privileges rather than the way to become an *actual* son or daughter of God. Many view themselves to be God's sons- and daughters-*in-law* rather than actual children of the Father.

The truth is, to those who are united to Christ, God has given the "right to become children of God, who were born, not of blood nor of the will of the flesh nor of the will of man, but of God" (John 1:12-13). In other words, the Father himself has chosen and called you in his loving grace to be spiritually born of *him*. In Christ you are a child of God not only legally but really. This is, according to Paul, in full "accordance with his [the Father's] pleasure and will—to the praise of his glorious grace, which he has freely given us *in* the One he loves" (Ephesians 1:5-6, NIV, emphasis added). Who is the One he loves? Jesus Christ. Where do we become children of God? *In* Christ. See, you're getting it!

Just as the Holy Spirit, the loving bond between the Father and the Son, rested on Jesus at his baptism, all those who are united to Christ have received the *exact same* Holy Spirit, whereby we can now cry "Abba! Father!" (Romans 8:15). The Father's affirmation of Christ's natural sonship (with all of its rights and privileges) now directly applies to all those who have been united to his Son by grace. And how could it not be? To be united to the Son of God by the Spirit of God, and somehow not be a full and complete son or daughter of God ourselves, would be to deny the sonship of Christ and undermine the person and work of the Holy Spirit!

Through the Holy Spirit, the Father takes what is most precious to Christ and makes it ours (John 16:14). In this way, we are not merely *declared* to be sons and daughters by the Spirit, we have *received* the Spirit of sonship *himself* (Galatians 4:6; Romans 8:15). Therefore, being a child of God is not just a legal act, but an intensely relational, intimate, and personal fact. This is why John will say, "See what great love the Father has lavished on us, that we should be called children of God! And that is what we are!" (1 John 3:1, NIV). The supreme benefit of being united to Christ is not that we share in his authority or anointing, or that we are merely deemed to be righteous and forgiven. Instead, being united to Christ affords us the grace by which we are now fully (and forever) included and accepted into God's family as true sons and daughters. This is the heart of divine adoption.

Knowing ourselves to be actual sons and daughters of God is central to our identity in Christ. In the words of J. I. Packer, adoption is *the highest privilege that the gospel offers.*[1] In fact, being a child of God is the most real thing about us. It is what defines every aspect of our being. If this is true, then why is it that most Christians today, in the words of George MacDonald, find that "the hardest . . . thing in the world is to cry Father! from a full heart"?[2] Certainly this inability can be attributed in part to the devastating effects of divorce, absentee fathers, and misguided masculinity that pervade our culture today. But I believe the *primary* reason so many devoted Christians cannot fully and confidently declare God as Father (and themselves as children of God) is because of the lack of emphasis and misunderstanding of divine adoption.[3] The problem is theological.

When expressions of the gospel fail to take into account our union with Christ, the gifts of Christ (particularly divine adoption) are presented as little more than impersonal declarations of a distant God.[4] The effects of this deistic and declarative understanding of God and his gifts are beyond catastrophic to the people of God. God is seen not as a loving, engaged, and ever-present Father but as an impersonal and uninterested adoptive parent of children who are only *technically* his. The resulting "little orphan Annie" syndrome cultivates a life riddled with the constant fear of abandonment, resulting in legalism, moralism, or something worse. And if people do not believe that they are fully and completely children of God, they have little recourse when they fall short of their own striving: How can we cry "Father!" from a full heart if we believe our Father doesn't really care and that he may throw us away at any moment? It's only when we awaken to our union with the one true Son of God that we are able to finally (and fully) delight in God as *our* gentle and compassionate Father, who is remarkably fond of us. In the words of J. I. Packer:

> If you want to judge how well a person understands Christianity, find out how much he makes of the thought of being God's child, and having God as his Father. If this is not the thought that prompts and controls his worship and prayers and his whole outlook on life, it means that he does not understand Christianity very well at all. . . . [For] our understanding of Christianity cannot be better than our grasp of adoption.[5]

Therefore, just as Jesus' natural sonship defined his life and ministry, so should our divine adoption by grace define who we are as sons and daughters of God in Christ. If not, then we may not understand Christianity very well.

## "WHOM I LOVE": HEARING THE "YES" OF THE FATHER

One of the questions my sister and I used to pester our parents with when we were growing up was, "Which one of us do you love the most?" My father would always reply, "The both of you."

"But Dad," I would counter, "which one is it? Me or Amy?"

He would normally say, "Yes."

When it comes to love—even God's love—it's natural to think in terms of a sum total equation. For instance, if God loves "the world" and there are roughly seven billion people living on the planet, then you and I are entitled to roughly 1/7,000,000,000th of God's love, right? Is that enough love for you? No. That's crazy. God loves everyone 100 percent. How could he not? His love knows no limits and knows no boundaries. As an infinite God he has an infinite capacity of love, allowing him to give 100 percent of his affection and 100 percent of his attention to every single person on the planet every single second of every single day! This means that right now as you read these words, God's complete and utter focus is on you. But not only you, but your spouse, your wayward child, your loved ones, and yes, even your enemies. Hard to believe? It is. But God is that big—and that small. Listen to how the apostle Paul described God's ineffable love:

For this reason I bow my knees before the Father . . .
that according to the riches of his glory he may grant
you to be strengthened with power through his Spirit
in your inner being, so that Christ may dwell in your
hearts through faith—that you, being rooted and
grounded in love, may have strength to comprehend
with all the saints what is the *breadth and length and
height and depth, and to know the love of Christ that
surpasses knowledge,* that you may be filled with all
the fullness of God.

EPHESIANS 3:14,16-19, EMPHASIS ADDED

Did you hear that? God's love does not operate as a
sum total game. Because you and I have been united to the
supreme object of the Father's love and affection—the person
of Jesus Christ—each adopted child of God is the *most-loved*
of God's children. We are loved with the *very same love* with
which the Father has eternally loved his own Son.

*But how can this be?* we protest. *Jesus is perfect and we are
sinful! The Son is eternal and we are mere mortals! How can
God love us sinners as much as he loves Christ himself?* This is
precisely what is so outrageous about our union with Christ:
God's love and acceptance of us is based not on individual
performance or privilege, but on the individual person of
Jesus Christ. If we are united to Christ, according to the
apostle Paul, we have been "baptized by one Spirit so as to
form one body" (1 Corinthians 12:13, NIV), thereby sharing in the "same love" (Philippians 2:2) between the Father

and the Son. The contradiction would be for someone to be joined to the person of Christ and somehow claim that the Father loves Christ more, and them less! Or somehow consider themselves to be "less loved" than another brother or sister in Christ. Since Christ himself is not divided, neither is the Father's love for all those united to Christ Jesus. All the promises God has made (including the promise that the Father would love us even as he loved the Son) are all "Yes" *in Christ* (see 2 Corinthians 1:20). This the Father "has freely given us *in* the One he loves" (Ephesians 1:6, NIV, emphasis added).

Theologian Clark Pinnock once noted that "if salvation is union, conversion is awakening to love."[6] The pinch of this definition is that until we understand salvation as union with Christ, we will remain unconverted to the reality of our identity as the beloved. We will continue to strive and not rest. We will continue to doubt and not believe. We will continue to hunger and thirst but never be filled. We will continue to peer into the all-consuming love between the Father and the Son but never experience what it means to be the beloved ourselves. In short, we will continue to live our lives as orphans, unaware of how deeply and passionately we are loved of *our* Father. In the haunting yet hope-filled words of Fil Anderson,

Until the unlimited, unbridled and unrelenting love of God takes root in our life, until God's reckless pursuit of us captures our imagination, until our

head knowledge of God settles into our heart
through pure grace, nothing really changes.[7]

Everything changes, however, as we awaken to our union
with Christ and who we are as the most loved of God. We
begin to experience a life lived in restful confidence, divorced
from endless striving and constant doubt. We have the courage to own up to our past, accept our present, and hope
for a better tomorrow. Being the beloved allows us to come
clean and admit (finally!) that we aren't as bad as we think
(we're worse), but we are loved more than we can ever imagine. Understanding ourselves to be the beloved of God is the
indispensable reality of our identity that gives us the strength
to overcome every failure, every criticism, every breakup,
every setback, and every rejection. It affords us, in the words
of Richard Rohr, "the safety, the spaciousness, and the scary
freedom to be *who* we are, *all* that we are, *more* than we are,
and *less* than we are."[8] Who we are is the beloved.

## "WITH HIM I AM WELL PLEASED": RECEIVING THE ETERNAL SMILE OF GOD

A few years ago, I was asked by a spiritual mentor of mine to
draw a picture of how I thought God viewed me. The assignment seemed simple enough. However, when I finally sat
down with pencil and paper, the simple assignment turned
into an eye-opening experience. After staring at a blank piece
of paper for several minutes, this is what I sketched. (Don't
snicker.)

That's me—the weird-looking one on his knees in humble worship. Surrounding me are all the things that seemed to define me at the time. The first, starting from left to right (and in no particular order), is my temper. After that, my Tourette's, my pride, my lack of prayer, my spotty Bible reading, my lusts, my irregular church attendance, my narcissism, my insecurities, and finally, my selfishness.

Above me I drew three faces. Each face represented the way I understood God to see me in light of all that was before him. One face is smiling, another is stoic, and the one to the right is frowning. Originally, I wanted to draw a line connecting one of the faces to me. But when I went to do so, I sat motionless. *Which one is it?* I thought. *Is God happy, stoic, or upset with what he sees?* I honestly couldn't answer the question, so I stopped.

When I turned in my assignment, my mentor asked me to explain what I drew. Then he snatched the picture from my hand, took a big black Sharpie, and drew a huge cross that completely covered me and everything that surrounded me. "Which face is it now?" my mentor asked.

Point made.

When you look at God looking at you (and all that seems to identify you), what do you see? Utter delight? Supreme pleasure? An affirming smile? Do you see a frown? A grimace? Or worse, indifference and indecisiveness? The majority of Christians I've met over the years believe (either consciously or unconsciously) that God's delight for them is subject to change day by day, hour by hour, moment by moment—and yes, sin by sin. They may be confident to a degree that God loves and accepts them, but they are less confident that God consistently delights in them no matter what. In this way, many Christians are left wondering which God they are dealing with and how this God *actually* feels about them.

While it is true that God is grieved by our sin and does not approve of our sin and rebellion, this does not mean that God ceases to be fully delighted in us as his beloved children. When God looks at us, his delight is not determined by what we do but by *who we are*. And if we have been united to Christ, the very same pleasure and fondness God eternally has for his only begotten Son is ours. All of it. Every. Single. Bit.

If you are in Christ, you do not have to picture a God trying to figure out how he feels about you at any given moment. Instead, you can see an eternal Father who rejoices over us "with gladness" and exults over us "with loud singing" (Zephaniah 3:17). This stands in complete contrast to the moody, irritable, capricious, passive-aggressive God many of us see, a God who demonstrates his displeasure by taking away his delight and removing his approval of us whenever we fail.

Failure and even disobedience are inevitable on this side of eternity. It is precisely *because* God fully delights in us as his children that he corrects, reproves, and disciplines us when we fail or disobey. This is why the Bible says, "The LORD reproves him whom he loves, as a father the son in whom he delights" (Proverbs 3:12). Even when God corrects and disciplines us, he *always* does so out of complete love and because of his absolute delight in us as his children.

For example, my three young sons disobey me countless times a day. (Usually, they do as I ask.) When I tell one of them, "Ryan, pick up your socks," "Cole, share with your brother," "Jack, don't hit Ryan," and they don't obey, I don't shout, "I don't like you anymore!" and stomp back to my room where I stay until my displeasure for them blows over. Heavens, no. Instead, *because* I delight in them, I correct their behavior, all the while attempting to show them how much they are pleasing to me as my boys. I may not be pleased with what they do or how they act, but I'm always and forever pleased with who they are as my children. They are my supreme joy and incomprehensible delight; even in times of disobedience, they are mine!

The American Quaker and abolitionist John Greenleaf Whittier once said, "The smile of God is Victory."[9] When you live with the eternal smile of God over your life, you no longer live in defeat. You begin to see life differently. You recognize the warmth the sun brings to your face. You notice colors, sounds, and smells that somehow previously escaped your attention. Food regains its taste. Living under the smile of God allows you to walk more confidently and sleep more comfortably. Your shoulders relax and you sit with your legs crossed more often. You breathe deeper and take life a little easier. But most of all, when you walk in the complete delight of your Father, you can begin to delight in God once again as *your* Father. Constant confession turns into constant praise and adoration. Fear gives way to faith. Doubt turns into assurance. Insecurity is replaced with security. Frightened rebellion gives way to willful obedience. You discover that all along there was nothing you had to prove to God, to others, and *especially* to yourself. You realize that at no point, ever, was the Father's love, acceptance, and delight at stake or in question. Moreover, as you begin to delight in the Father, you begin to delight once again in your spouse, your children, and your family. And before you know it, you begin to delight in yourself once again—as God's beloved.

## DISCUSSION QUESTIONS

1. *Do you believe that you are God's child, whom he loves, and in whom he is well pleased? Be brave and explain.*
2. *What are the things we root our identities in other than who we are in Christ? What about you? What are the*

top three things in your life (or your past) that attempt to define you today?

3. In the space below, draw a picture of how you think God views you. Be honest and draw what you really think and feel.

# 8

# THE SPIRITUAL DISCIPLINES: PARADIGM SHIFT

*If our gospel does not free the individual for a unique life of*
*spiritual adventure in living with God daily, we simply have*
*not entered fully into the good news that Jesus brought.*

DALLAS WILLARD, *HEARING GOD*

WHEN MONICA AND I MARRIED in June 2002, we stood before God and others and somehow became "one flesh." Over the last fourteen years, we have argued, fought, loved, and laughed. We have moved five times, had three children, and changed jobs four times between the both of us. We have watched one another grow a little older, move a little slower, and gain a few inches on our waists (especially me!). While many things about us and our relationship have changed, one thing has remained the same over the years—our union.

By God's grace, the union established between us in 2002 is the very same union we share today. Married life, as we have come to understand it, is not the continual process by which we draw closer to one another. Why? Because we are already as close as we can possibly get to each other—we are one! Instead, we have found that the joy of marriage is the progressive deepening of our awareness, appreciation, and enjoyment of the perfect union we already have. This deepening comes as a result of living our ordinary lives with one another—where we face everyday trials and where we celebrate occasional victories. We come to realize the depth of our union through the ordinary and the mundane, as well as through the extraordinary and the glorious. And I can tell you, we have only scratched the surface of the mysterious union that defines our relationship.

In the same way, the day you gave your life to Christ, you became perfectly one with him. In that moment, a brand-new creation was formed (see 2 Corinthians 5:17). If this is true, then the Christian life is less about trying to "press into" a God who is outside of you and more about delving deeper into the reality of the perfect union you already have with God the Father, Son, and Holy Spirit. In this way, according to Richard Rohr, the starting point of the spiritual disciplines is one of being "already there."[1] Where is *there*? In Christ!

If this is true, then our motivation, approach, and practice of "doing" prayer, Bible reading, worship, and the like change dramatically. It's a complete paradigm shift. Instead of practicing the spiritual disciplines as an attempt to "draw close" to God or earn his affection, we are free to rest in and savor the perfect union we already have with God. In this way, the Christian life is the ongoing deepening of our awareness, appreciation, and enjoyment of the perfect union we already have with the Father, Son, and Holy Spirit. This deepening is on God's time and is solely God's work.

Therefore, in the words of my friend and mentor Fil Anderson, "growing spiritually" is like "working on your tan." There is a work for us to do, but that work is to simply position ourselves so that Christ might do what he naturally does—transform us into the likeness of himself. This is why Richard Foster, in his classic work *A Celebration of Discipline*, speaks of the disciplines as "the path of disciplined grace." Prayer, Scripture reading, silence, solitude—they are each a grace because they are free. Yet they are disciplines because "there is something for us to do."[2] And that "something" has more to do with intentional *positioning* than constant *pressing*; more to do with *conformity* to Christ than *proximity* to him.

How can we position ourselves so that we might "be conformed to the image" of Christ (Romans 8:29)? What are the ways we can deepen and expand into the endless mystery of our union with the Father, Son, and Spirit? Corporate and private Bible reading and meditating on the Scriptures are critical in deepening our union with Christ. So is prayer. But with so many believers struggling to read their Bible and pray,[3] are there complementary disciplines that can help lead us into an awareness of God's ever-now presence in our lives? Are there things we can be doing until the Holy Spirit stirs in us a longing for intentional Scripture reading and prayer? In this chapter, we will consider four such disciplines:

› Doing Nothing
› Praying Simply
› Staying Attentive
› Being Led

## DOING NOTHING: THE DISCIPLINE OF FAITH

Jesus once said that unless a grain of wheat falls into the ground and dies, it cannot bear fruit (John 12:24). This is why a farmer, according to James, "waits for the precious fruit of the earth, being patient about it, until it receives the early and the late rains" (James 5:7). The Christian life, from beginning to end, is based on an utter dependence on Jesus Christ. United to Christ, we are dependent on him as the vine for everything we need for life and godliness. All too often, Christians seek to "grow spiritually" without realizing that the call of the spiritual life is first and foremost to abide in Christ. As Jesus said to his disciples, "Abide in me, and I in you. As the branch cannot bear fruit by itself, unless it abides in the vine, neither can you, unless you abide in me" (John 15:4).

So what does it mean to "abide" in Christ? In short, it means to do nothing. Zero. Zilch. Nada. The discipline of doing nothing is the first step in awakening to the mystery and wonder of our union with Christ. Watchman Nee, in his classic work *Sit, Walk, Stand*, argues that the first step in all spiritual growth is to "sit down and enjoy what God has done for us—not to set out to try and attain it for ourselves."[4] Since, after making purification of sins, Christ "sat down at the right hand of the Majesty on high" (Hebrews 1:3), all those who are united to Christ have now been made to sit with him. This is why Paul says that "in Christ" we have been "blessed . . . with every spiritual blessing" (Ephesians 1:3). Whatever is his is ours. Whatever he has accomplished is already accomplished for us and in us. Wherever he is, there we are. And where we are is "seated . . . with him in the heavenly places" right this second (Ephesians 2:6). What an unfathomable truth!

If we somehow skip the discipline of doing nothing, we will inevitably see our Christian life as a perpetual "pressing" into Christ instead of abiding in the intimacy we *already have* with and in Christ.

Theologically, it was out of nothing that the Eternal Word called all things into being. He did this so that all of creation might participate and abide *in him* through whom "all things hold together" (Colossians 1:17). When we do nothing, and assume the position of rest afforded to us in our union with Christ, we begin, in the words of German philosopher Paul Tillich, to "accept [our own] acceptance."[5]

This is hard work. It takes more faith to believe we are loved and accepted by God when we are doing nothing than when we are doing as much as we can for God. In his classic book *Abba's Child*, Brennan Manning likens the discipline of doing nothing with the settling of water:

> It takes time for the water to settle. Coming to interior stillness requires waiting. Any attempt to hasten the process only stirs up the water anew.
>
> Guilt feelings may arise immediately. The shadow self insinuates that you are selfish, wasting time, and evading the responsibilities of family, career, ministry, and community. [. . .] Theologian Edward Schillebeeckx wrote, ". . . silence with God has a value in itself and for its own sake, just because God is God. Failure to recognize the value of mere[ly] being with God, as the beloved, without doing anything, is to gouge the heart out of Christianity."[6]

When I first read this in *Abba's Child* years ago, I cried for nearly an hour straight. I had spent so much of my Christian life trying to "do" for God that I never learned how to simply settle and abide in Christ. But all spiritual growth begins with having the faith to simply be with the Father, as the beloved, without doing a single thing. It is in this posture that we begin to grow naturally.

What does abiding in Christ look like? Let me give you an image. This is an ultrasound picture of our second son, Cole, at eighteen weeks in the womb.

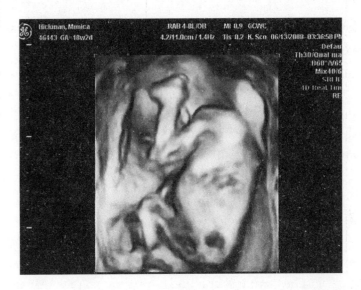

What is Cole doing to grow here? What is he doing to mature? Nothing. Think about it. He is simply abiding in the darkness of the womb of the one with whom he is united. There, he receives everything he needs for life. He is fully loved, fully accepted, and has nothing to prove. Nothing is at stake. Nothing is on the line. There is nothing for him to "do." The only thing required of him is to be. And yet somehow, mysteriously, he grows and matures. In the same way, the Christian life is meant to be lived as our natural lives are conceived: in the safety and spaciousness of God's all-encompassing love.

Being the beloved of God is not something you do. It's an internal posture of being. It's having the faith that somehow, someway, despite what you (and others) think of yourself, you are the utter delight of God the Father. It's believing that

God gets more glory out of your simple presence in life than your steadfast performance.

For this reason, doing nothing is the most frightening, vulnerable, and illogical thing you can do. Human logic says that you are loved because you are *valuable*. You bring something to the table—good looks, talents, popularity. But God's love is illogical, according to our notions of logic. God's love declares us valuable because we are *loved*. Human logic is not the ground where faith is cultivated. Real, lasting faith is cultivated when we are confronted with the illogical love God has for us. This is why Jesus tells us to "find a quiet, secluded place so you won't be tempted to role-play before God. Just be there as simply and honestly as you can manage. The focus will shift from you to God, and you will begin to sense his grace" (Matthew 6:6, MSG). So grab a spot and get to "work" on your tan.

## PRAYING SIMPLY: THE DISCIPLINE OF PRACTICING THE PRESENCE OF GOD

Prayer is critical to deepening the joy and wonder of our union with Christ. Jesus instructs his disciples (and us) how to pray with these words:

> Our Father in heaven,
> Reveal who you are.
> Set the world right;
> Do what's best—
> > as above, so below.

Keep us alive with three square meals.
Keep us forgiven with you and forgiving others.
Keep us safe from ourselves and the Devil.
You're in charge!
You can do anything you want!
You're ablaze in beauty!
    Yes. Yes. Yes.

MATTHEW 6:9-13, MSG

The Lord's Prayer is known for its semantic wonder. And the words themselves are beautiful! But what if, in focusing on the words, we have missed the point? I find it interesting that in teaching his disciples how to pray, Jesus models for them a thirty-second prayer. Time it yourself! It's as if Jesus was interested more in the *simplicity* of the prayer than in its *semantics*. The language Jesus uses is ordinary. The sentences he strings together are so simple they are childlike. And somehow, when we pray, this is how we are to do so—simply.

The reason we can pray simply, according to Jesus, is not because God is in a hurry. It's not because he knew we would be so busy that we'd have to pray in short, quick sentences. No, Jesus instructs us to pray in a simple childlike manner because God is our *Father*. And as our Father, he already knows what you and I need and when we need it. If this is true, how could we *not* pray simply? Therefore, prayer is more about *who we are praying to* than *what we are saying*. It's about trusting in who God is rather than trying to convince

God with our many words. This is precisely what Jesus says in the verses leading up to the Lord's Prayer:

> The world is full of so-called prayer warriors who are prayer-ignorant. They're full of formulas and programs and advice, peddling techniques for getting what you want from God. Don't fall for that nonsense. This is your Father you are dealing with, and he knows better than you what you need. With a God like this loving you, you can pray very simply.
> MATTHEW 6:7-8, MSG

For much of my life, my prayers have been marked by anything but simplicity. Formulas, prescriptions, and certain postures complicated and cluttered my attempts. My "prayer life" was an ongoing endeavor to string together emotionally charged words and phrases in order to clearly communicate my feelings to God. I was convinced that if I could find the right words that moved my own heart (either to remorse or thankfulness), somehow God would likewise be moved by my emotional eloquence and either forgive or rejoice with me. Because of this, I found myself speaking to God as if he needed to be persuaded to listen to me. In the end, prayer felt more like pleading with a disgruntled DMV worker than communicating with my loving Father.

Because we are united to Christ, prayer should be the simplest and most effortless thing we do. Wherever we are, whatever we do, Christ is present. Prayer, then, is the process by which we awaken to, acknowledge, and abide in Christ's ever-now presence in us—and our never-ending presence in him. Our ability to freely and easily commune with Christ and abide in his presence is one of the most freeing aspects of our union with Christ.

In the seventeenth century, a man by the name of Nicolas Herman understood prayer to be simply abiding in and enjoying the presence of God. Born into poverty in eastern France, Nicolas joined the army as a young man and fought in the Thirty Years' War. After suffering an injury, Nicolas joined the Discalced Carmelite Priory in Paris. Because he was not educated to be a minister, Nicolas served the priory as a lay brother and took for himself the name "Lawrence of the Resurrection." For nearly the entire rest of his life, "Brother Lawrence" (as he was known) worked as a cook within the monastery.

Due to the heavy workload, Brother Lawrence found it almost impossible to attend to his daily prayers. Instead, he decided to marry his everyday, mundane life (boiling eggs, cleaning the dishes, mopping the floor) to an internal posture of prayer. In this way, whatever Brother Lawrence did, he did with, through, and in Christ. This became known as "the practice of the presence of God." In the book that carries the same name, Joseph de Beaufort described the "prayer life" of Brother Lawrence as "nothing else but a sense of the presence of God, his soul being at that time insensible to everything but Divine Love." Brother Lawrence, in his own words, admitted that he ceased all forms of devotion and set prayers except those to which my state requires. I make it my priority to persevere in His holy presence, wherein I maintain a simple attention and a fond regard for God . . . an habitual, silent, and private conversation of the soul with God.[7]

In this way, Brother Lawrence prayed "without ceasing" (1 Thessalonians 5:17). The focus of his prayer was not speaking words to God but continually delighting in and adoring the divine presence of God.

Like the discipline of doing nothing, the discipline of praying simply requires a great deal of faith. It is difficult to pray simple words, phrases, or nothing at all and believe that our Father is intimately attuned to our needs, that he completely hears and fully understands. I have found that the more simply we are able to pray, the more we prove God to be our Father and ourselves his beloved children.

Back when our second son, Cole, was learning how to walk, I was sitting in the living room early one morning (attempting) to pray. I was stumbling over my words, upset at myself for having such a hard time, when all of a sudden I heard the pitter-patter of little feet sprinting in the darkness down the hall. Cole had somehow climbed out of his crib and was peeking at me from around the corner. I smiled and acknowledged his presence while motioning for him to climb onto my lap. As we sat together in the dark, Cole's attention turned toward my bagel, sitting on the coffee table in front of me. Without saying a word, Cole pointed to the bagel, then pointed to his open mouth. Nothing else needed to be "said." I knew exactly what my son wanted. I nodded playfully, leaned over, and handed Cole my bagel. He chuckled, lay back in my arms, and took a bite.

That's the type of prayer God longs for; that is simple prayer.

Since that morning, I have made a practice of identifying certain wants, needs, and desires, and internally "pointing" at them throughout the day. Usually I verbalize these to God as well, but there have been days where I've been too exhausted, stressed, or downright lazy to say anything. In those moments, I'll envision whatever it is I need to offer to God, and like Cole, I'll silently "point" to it in my spirit. There have been times I've sat through entire business meetings with an imaginary finger pointing directly at whatever was causing me anxiety, fear, or joy that day. And every time (whether I realize it or not), the Father nods his head and says, "I know. I've got it."

Just because prayer is simple does not mean it is not profound. I had a Catholic friend say to me once, "Dave, I've found that the hardest prayer to pray and believe is, 'In the name of the Father, and of the Son, and of the Holy Spirit, Amen.'" In the Orthodox tradition, the "Jesus Prayer" is the way many practice the presence of God: "Lord Jesus Christ, Son of God, have mercy on me, a sinner." Such prayers of the heart can be said throughout the day. Many make these prayers a part of their breathing: They inhale while praying, "Lord Jesus Christ, Son of God," and as they exhale, they pray, "Have mercy on me, a sinner." Other prayers of the heart may come directly from the Scriptures, or they may simply reinforce the truth of Scripture. Some of these simple prayers include:

› Glory be to the Father, and to the Son, and to the Holy Spirit.
› Worthy is the Lamb, who was slain.
› In you I live, move, and have my being.
› Nothing is at stake. I have nothing to prove. I am yours.
› Abba, I belong to you.

While I have a deep appreciation for beautifully worded prayers (and attempt to express them on occasion), I'm convinced that the prayer the Father longs for is one of childlike simplicity flowing from a heart of confidence and trust in the One who knows us better and more intimately than we know ourselves. Don't fall for the nonsense. Your Father already knows what you need before you ask. Therefore, pray simply.

## STAYING ATTENTIVE: THE DISCIPLINE OF BEING AWARE

In his book *Everything Belongs*, Richard Rohr makes the case for being aware of God's presence in our lives:

We cannot attain the presence of God because
we're already totally in the presence of God. What's

absent is awareness. Little do we realize that God is maintaining us in existence with every breath we take. As we take another it means that God is choosing us now and now and now.[8]

It's fascinating to think that, united to Christ, we are completely surrounded by (and consumed with) the *full* presence of God every hour, every second, of every day. If this is true, then the question is not whether God is fully present in our lives, but if we are living lives fully aware of God's presence. No wonder the psalmist prayed, "Open my eyes, that I may behold" (Psalm 119:18). The discipline of being attentive is simply that—the practice of being awake and aware so that we may behold God's all-encompassing presence in our lives.

Just yesterday, as I packed Ryan and Cole's lunches, I placed a note inside each that read, "I love you. Enjoy! —Dad." The note was simple but intentional. Picking up the boys later that day, I asked, "Did you see my love letter?" Cole did; Ryan didn't. I'm afraid I'm more like Ryan than Cole most days. I scurry from one meeting to the next, one appointment to the other, all the while running right past the simple "love letters" God intentionally places in my path to prove he is fully present and completely engaged in my life. No wonder loneliness and isolation so often pervade my soul.

Despite our inattentiveness, though, our Father is constantly surrounding us with both general and specific reminders of his love and grace. Generally speaking, as discussed in chapter 3, all of creation confronts us with a God who is eternal in power (see Romans 1:20) and mindful in his care (see Psalm 8). This is precisely why the Scriptures instruct us to "look," "gaze," and "watch." In other words, to be conscious—wide awake to God's presence and provision in our lives, our neighbors' lives, and the world around us.

The word Jesus liked to use was *consider* (in Greek, *manthano*, meaning "to observe closely"). Jesus implores his disciples in Matthew 6:28-30:

> Consider the lilies of the field, how they grow: they neither toil nor spin, yet I tell you, even Solomon in all his glory was not arrayed like one of these. But if God so clothes the grass of the field, which today is alive and tomorrow is thrown into the oven, will he not much more clothe you, O you of little faith?

Jesus could have very well lamented, "O you of little attention!" Look around! Open your eyes! Observe closely! Pay attention to all the intentional ways God cares for creation, and specifically you! Looking back over his life, my friend (and fellow Charlottean) Leighton Ford observed in his book *The Attentive Life*:

> If the *first* part of my own journey involved *longing*, the *second* has encompassed mainly *looking*—coming to terms with important parts of my soul, bringing my real self before the real God, and discovering prayer, as Simone Weil put it, as "absolute attention."[9]

For the better part of my life, I too have lived with such a great longing to be close to God that I failed to look (consider) just how close God has been (and continues to be) in my life. Blinded by doing, I became unaware of all that God was doing in and around me.[10] My life, in the spirit of Leighton's insight above, was one of *striving* instead of *seeing*, *attaining* instead of *attentiveness*, *pressing* instead of *pondering*, *chasing* hard instead of stopping to *consider*. But after awakening to (and embracing) my union with Christ, my mind and emotions were freed from the blinders of striving and performance. By embracing a God who is closer than close, I woke to the many ways God's presence inundates my life. And the same can happen for you as you awaken to *your* union with Christ.

Many times through the day a breeze or the warmth of the sun will stop me, reminding me of God's refreshing and warming presence in my life. I've sat in wonder during thunderstorms marveling at how God is not like me—how he is much bigger and stronger than I am. The smell of magnolia trees blooming on a spring day or the fragrance of rhododendrons during a hike will draw my attention to the sweetness of our God.

Most of all, I've come to see the presence of Christ in others as the greatest of all "icons" showing forth God's presence on earth. In the Catholic tradition, the Eucharist (as the body of Christ) is placed in a "monstrance" to be viewed and admired. This is referred to as eucharistic adoration. In doing this, our Catholic friends are not "worshiping the bread," as some accuse, but savoring who they understand the bread to contain—the presence of Jesus. In a similar way, I have come to view and savor Christ's presence in those I interact with throughout the day. I'll admire their smile, eyes, and unique mannerisms and consider the remarkable truth of "Christ in [us], the hope of glory" (Colossians 1:27). In doing this, I am not worshiping people but sitting in awe of a God who dwells in his people, the body of Christ.

Not only are we to consider God's *general* presence in the world, but we are to be on the lookout for the *specific* ways in which God wants to express his individual love and care in our lives.

In his book *Running on Empty*, Fil Anderson writes, "[I believe] God wants to meet us in some exacting way that shows how deep is the love in his heart for us."[11] When I first read this, I was struck with Fil's claim. The God of the universe, the Ancient of Days, wants to *specifically* meet me in some *exact* way to demonstrate his love for me? I felt much like David when he said,

> When I consider your heavens,
>     the work of your fingers,
> the moon and the stars,
>     which you have set in place,
> what is mankind that you are mindful of them,
>     human beings that you care for them?
> PSALM 8:3-4, NIV

The truth is, God is not only mindful of creation, he is personally mindful of us, desiring to meet us in some *exact way* to show that he is present in our lives and that he cares. We just have to be attentive—ready to acknowledge (and receive) the specific gift of the affirmation of his attention.

As I shared in chapter 6, I have lived (and wrestled) with Tourette's syndrome ever since I can remember. Neurologically, the chemicals that carry nerve signals from cell to cell in my brain (called neurotransmitters) are unbalanced, causing me to "tic." This imbalance contributes not only to Tourette's but also to other disorders such as anxiety and depression. For years (well, decades) I have lived with an impending sense of doom over my life. Depression and anxiety lorded over me, making it hard some days to go outside, brush my teeth, or even get out of bed. While asleep at night, I would sweat profusely. Upon waking, my anxiety and depression would immediately manifest in what my doctor later diagnosed as "anxiety-induced vomiting." For years, I dreaded the day ahead and despised the coming of morning. The only time I felt at peace was when I was asleep—which isn't much of a life at all. I longed for a new day to dawn, a day when I could wake with joy and peace.

Friends and family encouraged me to "get on medication," but I was too stubborn. I was convinced that I could pull myself together and eventually become joyful and carefree on my own. That day never came. Several years ago, after suffering a severe panic attack in the middle of the night, I finally admitted defeat and decided to give medication a try. It took a few days to get in my system. But after a week or so, the fog lifted and the anxiety-induced vomiting stopped.

One morning in particular, I remember, I woke up with an unusual sense of peace and hope. *It's a brand-new day*, I said to myself as I rolled out of bed. I hopped in the shower, put on my favorite Pandora channel (Noah Gundersen), and began thanking God for the healing I was experiencing. Just then, I heard a song playing that I had never heard. Intrigued, I listened closely and couldn't believe my ears:

*Some kind of magic*
*Happens late at night*
*When the moon smiles down at me*
*And bathes me in its light*

*I fell asleep beneath you*
*In the tall blades of grass*
*When I woke the world was new*
*I never had to ask*

*It's a brand new day*
*The sun is shining*
*It's a brand new day*
*For the first time in such a long long time*
*I know, I'll be ok*

JOSHUA RADIN, "BRAND NEW DAY"

Thankfulness flooded my heart. Hope washed over me. I wept like a child—so much so that I couldn't tell where the water from the shower ended and my tears began. Call it what you want. Chance? Irony? Happenstance? Not for me. Nooo sir. I am convinced that God (in all of his compassion and empathy) somehow allowed that *exact* song to play at that *exact* time so he might specifically show me (as his boy) that he was (and had always been) present in my suffering, and that a brand-new day had in fact dawned. Call me crazy if you want, but it's been a brand-new day ever since.[12]

How about you? Are you "doing" for God or being attentive to what God is already doing in your life? In what unique area of your life do you need God to specifically meet you? What part of your life lords over you with a sense of doom? Stop. Look around. Consider. Be attentive. Stay on the lookout for expressions of God's forever care that surround you, and be expectant for your Father to meet you in some exact way to assure you that he loves you and is present with you. He's there with you right now, closer than you are to yourself.

## BEING LED: THE DISCIPLINE OF FOLLOWING

Our union with Christ is a mystery that we will never fully understand this side of eternity. Luckily, there are those who have stopped long enough to sink into the bright abyss of its beauty and wonder. In doing so, they can help guide, lead, and direct us into the depths and wonder of our own union with Christ—if we are willing (and desperate enough) to follow.

After my panic attack, I turned to two people—Fil Anderson and Mike Moses Sr. I first met Fil during his years with Young Life; I was a volunteer leader, and he was the camp speaker at Windy Gap (a Young Life camp in North

Carolina). What drew me to Fil was his tender heart and his insatiable love for Jesus. Having practiced the presence of God for decades, Fil emanates Jesus though his person. When I came to the end of myself, Fil was there, gracious enough to sit with me once a month for a little over an hour. Just being with Fil, doing nothing but talking (and watching him cry), awakened me to Christ's presence in my life. Fil helped me navigate the still-virgin soil of my union with Christ through suggesting prayers and Bible verses, and overseeing personal retreats. He pointed out the cliffs of apathy and antinomianism (a rejection of moral obligations) off which some have fallen in the process of exploring their freedom in Christ.

One time while sitting with Fil, I described union with Christ like being dropped onto a pristine, sandy-white beach with no footprints to follow. Union with Christ was uncharted territory for me. There were no expectations, no laws, no rules—only freedom. How should I act? How should I pray? How should I read the Scriptures? How should I love? *What do I do? What would Jesus want me to do in this new life of union with him?*

With hot tears pooling in his eyes, Fil said, "I think Jesus would say, 'What do you want to do?'" His answer was like a foreign language. Yet I knew he was right.

Another time, after getting lost and receiving a speeding ticket on my drive to see him, I sat in Fil's office, livid, consumed with anger and self-hatred. "Why am I so angry?" I voiced.

Fil immediately leaned forward and said, "Maybe because God loves you so much."

When you are guided by someone who has already delved into the depths in which you are looking, much can be learned (and avoided). This is why throughout the Gospels, Jesus invited his disciples to "follow" him.

Following someone else's direction shows both humility of spirit and desperation of heart. According to Jesus, it's only when we are poor in spirit that healing and comfort can come. Fil led me not only by being my friend but by providing me with notebooks' worth of his insights and learnings. His counsel awakened me to a new way of seeing God, myself, and the world around me—just by being with him and being humble enough to follow.

But more than any other person, it was Mike Moses Sr. who walked with me, cried with me, and directed me in understanding my union with Christ. Every Wednesday for a year, Mike listened intently to my story, heard my fears and doubts, and helped me to understand (and pity) my "false self" (the one who constantly tries to please God and others) and to embrace my true self in Christ. I have a white three-inch binder filled with printouts Mike gave me concerning the truths of my newfound identity as God's beloved. On the front of the binder I wrote, "My New Life." On the back I wrote, "Because my old one sucked!" Even as a born-again, Bible-believing Christian, it did.

Mike's vast experience and expertise in leading people to their true self (and to the true Jesus) continues to be one of the greatest gifts of my life. Like Fil, Mike gave me books to read, sermons to listen to, and Scriptures and prayers to instruct and mold me. Most of all, he gave me himself. Every time I would walk up the path leading to his front door, Mike would be outside waiting on me with two cups of coffee—one for him and the other for me. He would greet me with a massive hug and a compassionate smile. He offered his mountain house for me and my family to vacation at and introduced me to a bunch of "dead people" to read. Mike taught me how to be a "dropout"—to permanently leave behind the rat race of trying to please God and be pleasing to him. I'm grateful he did. Most of all, I'm thankful I was desperate enough to follow.

The discipline of being led involves the willingness to entrust yourself to someone else's care. It's acknowledging that you don't have all the answers and that you have much to learn (no matter your age or experience). Following these two men, I discovered my true self that Jesus cherished. The primary way this happened was simple—they reminded me of who I was in Christ (which is simply bragging on who Christ is) over and over and over until the Holy Spirit gave me the grace to believe it. That is spiritual direction.

The apostle Paul once wrote to his friends, "Be imitators of me, as I am of Christ" (1 Corinthians 11:1). Jesus instructed his disciples, saying, "Take my yoke upon you, and learn from me, for I am gentle and lowly in heart, and you will find rest for your souls" (Matthew 11:29). Learning from others (and being led by them) releases the crushing weight of trying to figure out life on your own. It affords us the comfort that comes from entrusting ourselves to someone else and their care. In short, it allows another person to lead the way. We just have to be willing to follow and be led.

—

The spiritual disciplines outlined in this chapter, while important, are still inadequate to sustain and nurture our identity in Christ. We need more. Specifically, we need each other. Cultivating our union with Christ is not an individual activity but the responsibility of a believing comm*unity* of people who know and love us. Created in God's image and participating in the life of the Trinity, we are designed for (and now defined by) "belonging," not just "being." We naturally long to experience (and express) our union with Christ in solidarity with others. But many of us feel isolated and alone in our faith, quietly suffering from a nagging and often unidentified discontent deep within our souls. Orphaned from (or by) the church, many are left to fend for themselves—scraping to spiritually nurture and sustain their faith. No wonder so many of us are left wanting. No wonder we yearn for more. No wonder we feel anemic in our faith.

But the comforting reality is, united to Christ, we share a "common-union" not just with the Trinity but with all those who have been united to Christ by faith. The early church simply called this the "communion of saints" —the common-unity among believers rooted in (and founded upon) our shared communion with Christ and one another. This communal family among believers is expressed in the New Testament as "the church."

But what is the church? What does it mean to be a part of the church? And more importantly, how does our union with Christ inform and guide our participation in the church? With these questions in mind, we now turn to the church and her mission in the world.

So, if you would, follow me.

## DISCUSSION QUESTIONS

1. *How would your motivation and approach to the spiritual disciplines change if you* really *believed you were already as close to Christ as possible? Explain.*

2. *Do you believe that "doing nothing" should be considered a spiritual discipline? Explain.*

3. *In one word, describe your prayer life. Did this chapter help redefine prayer for you? If so, how?*

4. *Share a time when God specifically made his loving presence and care known in your life.*

# 9

# THE CHURCH:
# THE BODY OF CHRIST

*One hundred religious persons knit into a unity by careful
organization do not constitute a church any more than eleven dead
men make a football team. The first requisite is life, always.*

A. W. TOZER, *MAN: THE DWELLING PLACE OF GOD*

A FEW YEARS AGO I decided to make myself available for an
entire week to listen to the stories of others. Since the majority
of my time in ministry had been standing *before* people teaching the Bible and telling *my* story, I figured it was time for me
to sit *with* people and listen to what *they* had to say—whatever
they had to say, however they wanted to say it. I had no agenda.
There were no hidden motives. Just the offer to sit and listen.

I posted the offer (and the dates) on Facebook and
Twitter, thinking only a handful of people might respond.
I was shocked, however, to discover that within a matter of
days, my calendar began to fill with back-to back one-hour
meetings. *Am I this cool, or are these people that desperate?*

(My head quickly deflated when my wife reminded me that my seventy-year-old mom still buys most of my clothes from Kohl's. Well, sometimes Ross Dress for Less.)

Over five days I sat with nearly twenty people—friends and strangers, young people and old people, Christians and agnostics—hearing stories of hope, courage, and faith, as well as stories of death, abuse, and lost love. Embedded in almost every story, one particular topic kept popping up. Some people began their story with it. Others built their story around it. Most people concluded their story with some sort of comment about it.

No, I'm not talking about the new iPhone. I'm talking about the church.

Day after day that week, I was struck with how the church was such a formative part of the lives of those sitting before me. Granted, I live in the Bible Belt, but many were born elsewhere. Regardless of where people were from, however, virtually everyone had *some* experience with the church and had *something* they wanted (needed) to say about it.

Most of the time, what they said began with the all-too-familiar words, "I used to go to church, but . . ." In working with people in their twenties and thirties for the last decade, I wasn't surprised by this lead-in. In fact, I have come to expect it. What I wasn't expecting, however, were the various ways in which my new friends finished the sentence:

> › Instead of finding community, I found condemnation.
> › When my world fell apart, no one seemed to care.

> I couldn't take the rules and hypocrisy.
> Worship was like a performance.
> Sermons were like lectures.
> It felt routine and lifeless.
> I lost interest.
> I'm done.

I could go on. But I won't.

As I listened to how the church "let down," "lost," or "failed" each person, a pixelated image began to form in my mind—a mosaic of sorts, comprised of the many detailed accounts of discontent and discouragement I heard that week. But no matter how hard I tried to step back and see the overall image, I couldn't seem to piece the mosaic together. *What's the image? A spoiled consumer? A high-maintenance person? Maybe a drama-filled American?*

I was driving home exhausted that Friday evening when the image finally came together. I envisioned a wounded lover. Ordinary, everyday people desperately longed to experience Jesus but experienced rejection instead. People deeply longed to love and be loved, know and be known, but were left isolated and alone. People *really wanted* to be a part of a community of faith, but were "done" trying to find what they were longing for. These people, as I have come to find out, are referred to as "the Dones."

The Dones, according to sociologists Josh Packard and Ashleigh Hope in their book *Church Refugees*, are faith-filled, lifelong Christians who, instead of giving up on their faith, have given up on church (or at least on going to church).[1] These are the Christians who, at some point or another, poured their time, talent, and treasure into the church, only to find themselves spewed back out. In the playful words of Neil Carter, these are the "been there and done that, and probably have a T-shirt (or thirty)"[2] category of Christians. These are the folks who arrived early to brew coffee, run sound, park cars, and greet people at the door. The Dones even include former pastors and church staff members. But now, for whatever reason, they have exited the same doors they used to welcome others through, with little if any desire to return. One such person is a young woman named Abby.

## ABBY'S STORY: TOO MUCH TO ASK?

I first met Abby during my weeklong marathon of meetings. Raised in a Christian home, Abby accepted Christ at an early age. "To this day," she told me, "nothing is more important than my relationship with Jesus." She was so taken by the love of Christ as a child that she devoted herself to developing her newfound relationship with him. This included regularly attending church with her family and being a leader in her youth group.

"I used to love going to church," Abby told me. But like so many of her "done" counterparts, her view of the church began to deteriorate in college. "Going to church began to seem routine and bland. I'd go wanting to experience Jesus, but the services seemed routine, cookie-cutter. I just lost interest."

I cast an inquisitive look. "What do you mean by 'cookie-cutter'?"

"Well," Abby said with a sigh, "all the churches I went to were virtually the same. We sing a few songs, the pastor gives a message, and everybody leaves and goes their separate ways. Even when I visited my church back home, I noticed the same thing. Don't get me wrong," she quickly continued. "I love being with everybody, singing the songs, and hearing the message. I just want more, I guess."

"What does 'more' look like for you?" I gently prodded.

"I don't know," she responded with a smile. "*Jesus?* The reason I wake up early, get ready, and drive to church is to experience the presence of Jesus with others. Again, the worship is really good and the sermon is challenging. I just want more—I don't know—substance. I want to know that the church is a part of a larger story in the world. I want to know that what we do in that hour matters. I want to experience Jesus deeply and express my faith with others whose faith matters to them. But when I go to church today, I see little passion and even less engagement between Christians. It's like everyone is an island. All I want is to be a part of a church that loves each other and experiences Jesus in a real way. *Is that too much to ask?*"

Her question stopped me. I wasn't sure how to respond. I had read what the Christian blogosphere had to say about people like Abby. I had heard countless pastors lamenting about the consumeristic mentality of many Christians today. I had sat privately with Christian leaders all over the nation

discussing the "entitled" mentality of the "younger generation." But the heart and passion with which Abby spoke was
far from consumeristic; her words were not laced with hostil-
ity for the church or a sense of entitlement. I could tell her
question came from her heart—a wounded heart filled with a
genuine desire for Jesus and a passion to belong to a church.

I shifted in my seat. "I guess it depends," I said pensively.

Abby sat silent—frozen with a palpable sense of anticipation and dread. I could tell my answer would either provide
hope or put a fork in her view of the church.

"On—on what?" Abby's eyes began filling with tears.

"On who you ask," I said with a grin.

Abby paused. I could see that she wasn't sure whether she
wanted to ask the next logical question.

"Well, what do *you* think?" she finally asked, wiping the
first tear from her cheek.

I didn't delay. "No. Not at all," I said. "It's not too much
to ask."

—

Over the years, I've thought a lot about Abby. More than
anything, I've thought about her question. What would I say
to her today? How would I *specifically* answer her question?
Is it really too much to ask of the church to be a place where
people love each other and experience Jesus in a real way?

If I had another hour with Abby, I would assure her that
while she may consider herself "done" with church, the

church (as well as Christ himself) isn't done with her. In fact, I would point out that she isn't a member of the Dones, but instead, one of many broken, battered, and wounded people who make up the mosaic of the church. I would tell her to take an uncomfortably long look in the mirror; there, in the midst of her longing and dissatisfaction, she might see herself for *what* she is, *whose* she is, and what (more like *whom*) she is a part of—the Wounded Body of Christ himself.

## THE BODY OF CHRIST

If you have spent any time around church (or church people, for that matter), you have probably heard the church described as "the body of Christ." But what does this phrase actually mean? Why is it important to understand the church as Christ's body? And how literally should Christians understand themselves to be a part of the body of Christ?

Throughout Paul's thirteen letters, the apostle consistently refers to the church as being the body of Christ. Writing to the church in Corinth, Paul says, "For in one Spirit we were all baptized *into one body*—Jews or Greeks, slaves or free— and all were made to drink of one Spirit. . . . Now *you are the body of Christ and individually members of it*" (1 Corinthians 12:13, 27, emphasis added).

According to Paul, the church has been united to the risen Christ in such a way that believers are now joined to his "body" and "individually members of it." Therefore, instead of some kind of ethereal or spiritual body, Paul describes the union between Christ and the church, in the words of theologian

Pierre Benoit, "as a kind of physical union of the body of the Christian with the individual body of Christ."[3] Benoit's words echo those of Cyril of Alexandria, who, writing in the fifth century, declared, "Since we are all united with the one Christ through His sacred body, and since we all receive Him who is one and indivisible into our own bodies, we ought to look upon our members as belonging to Him rather than to ourselves."[4]

But claiming that the church is somehow united to Christ's physical body and "individually members of it" raises an enormous question: *What type of union does the church share with Christ's physical body?* In other words, does the church somehow serve as (or replace) Christ's *literal* body here on earth? Or conversely, is the church so absorbed into Christ's own physical body that believers lose their distinctiveness?

Luckily, Paul does not leave us guessing. But he does leave us scratching our heads. While in prison, having suffered much physical pain and torture, the weary apostle paints his most sublime image of the church as the "bride of Christ."

## THE BRIDE OF CHRIST

Writing to the church in Ephesus, Paul leverages the mysterious one-flesh union between a husband and a wife to further clarify the nature of Christ's union with the church. Pointing back to Adam's union with Eve in the Garden, Paul poignantly (and physically) makes his case:

> Husbands, love your wives, as Christ loved the church
> and gave himself up for her. . . . In the same way

husbands should love their wives *as their own bodies.*
He who loves his wife loves himself. For no one ever
hated his own flesh, but nourishes and cherishes it,
just as Christ does the church, *because we are members
of his body.* "Therefore a man shall leave his father and
mother and hold fast to his wife, and the two shall
become one flesh." This mystery is profound, *and I
am saying that it refers to Christ and the church.*
EPHESIANS 5:25, 28-32, EMPHASIS ADDED

Just as a husband and wife are spiritually, emotionally,
and physically made "one flesh" in marriage and yet retain
their distinctiveness, so the church, according to Paul, is
made "one flesh" with the person of Christ. So, instead of
the church somehow replacing Christ's body or believers (or
Christ) losing their distinctiveness in their one-flesh union,
the church, according to Martin Luther, is

so cemented to Christ that [we] are as *one person,*
which cannot be separated but remains attached
to Him forever. . . . Thus Eph. 5:30 says: "We are
members of the body of Christ, of His flesh and
of His bones," in such a way that this faith couples
Christ and [the church] more intimately than a
husband is coupled to his wife.[5]

This one-flesh union, as we have seen, is afforded to the
church by the Holy Spirit, who, according to John Calvin,

"truly unites things separated by distance."[6] Through the work (and person) of the Holy Spirit, the church is so cemented to Christ that she is as one person with Christ *even though* he is presently "at the right hand of God" (Romans 8:34). In this way, according to Martin Luther, Christ and the church are "coupled." "Such is the nature of union with Christ," affirms Baptist theologian Augustus Strong. "It is this and this only which constitutes him as a Christian, and which makes possible a Christian church."[7]

While imagining yourself as the bride of Christ and sharing in a one-flesh union with him might sound a bit fanatical, remember Calvin's earlier words: "All that he [Christ] possesses is *nothing to us* until we grow into *one body* with him."[8] In other words, the church *has* to be united to Christ as a wife is united to her husband *and* a husband is united to his wife. If not, everything that belongs to Christ (salvation, forgiveness, eternal life) and everything that belongs to humanity (sin, transgression, iniquity) remains distinct to each person. In order for Christ to take and heal our sin in him, and for us to become the "righteousness of God" (2 Corinthians 5:21), Christ and the church *have to* be joined together in a one-flesh union.[9] According to Martin Luther, Christ takes upon himself what is ours and has given us what is his, so he has made our sins his own and has made his righteousness ours.[10] What an unfathomable truth. What love!

This "happy exchange,"[11] according to Luther, takes place at the altar of faith where we throw our life away in order to become "one person" with Jesus Christ, our divine husband.

In this way, the church is the body of Christ (and we individually are members of Christ's body) precisely because she has entered into a one-flesh union with Christ.

## CHRIST LOVES AND CARES FOR HIS BODY

Understanding the church to be united to Christ as his body in this way is critical for a number of reasons. For the sake of our purposes here, I'd like to briefly point out three.

First, being the body of Christ proves Christ's *personal love and care* for the church. Paul writes, "For no one ever hated his own flesh, but nourishes and cherishes it, just as Christ does the church, because we are members of his body" (Ephesians 5:29-30). Over the fourteen years of my marriage with Monica, we have discovered that our union is such that what we do to one another somehow affects us both individually. When I'm short, irritable, and argumentative, it not only hurts Monica, it somehow casts a deep gloom over my own soul. In the same way, when I love, nurture, and care for Monica (as I *love* to do to my own body), I am filled with happiness, joy, and security. Likewise, when Monica suffers, it's as if I am the one suffering. When I rejoice, Monica rejoices. When Monica grieves, I grieve right along with her.

United to Christ as his bride, we can be confident that Christ himself will cherish and care for us as he does his own body. When we suffer, we do not suffer alone; Christ himself suffers in, with, and through us. When we rejoice, Christ rejoices. Instead of a God who lays heavy burdens on us and throws our sins in our face, we have a divine husband who is as gentle with us as he is with himself. It's little wonder, then, that Jesus bids us to "yoke" ourselves to him, because he is "gentle and lowly in heart" (Matthew 11:29).

Second, being the body of Christ demonstrates his *sacrificial love* for the church. Paul writes, "Husbands, love your wives, as Christ loved the church and *gave himself up* for her" (Ephesians 5:25, emphasis added). The eternal Son of God, who existed in the beginning with God and was God, humbled himself in order to assume a human nature so that, in his body, you and I might be healed through his life and cleansed through his sacrificial death on the cross.[12] In this way, God the Father demonstrated his own love for us: "While we were still sinners, Christ died for us" (Romans 5:8).

Although we have hurt one another in the church, we can be confident that Christ *himself* was "pierced for our transgressions; he was crushed for our iniquities" (Isaiah 53:5). Out of the Father's great love for us, he "laid on [Christ] the iniquity of us all" (Isaiah 53:6). "Greater love," Jesus says, "has no one than this, that someone lay down his life for his friends" (John 15:13).

In giving himself up once and for all, Christ has established himself as the head of the church and is himself the Savior and supreme demonstration of the Father's love for us. For this reason, according to Paul, all believers everywhere should have "the same mindset" as that of Christ Jesus (Philippians 2:5, NIV): No matter how the church may have disappointed or wounded us, all believers, on the basis of Christ's sacrificial love, are called to sacrificially love *all* who are joined to his body. Therefore, believers are called to love one another *as* Christ himself (see Matthew 25:40). By virtue of our union with Christ, the way believers love and treat one another affects not only those in the church, but the one in whom the church is united—the person of Christ.

This does not mean that we must sacrifice ourselves for an institution or organization called "the church." What it does mean is that we are to surrender our expectations, desires, and wants in order to love, serve, and maintain the unity among the members of Christ's body ("the church"). This is why Paul, pointing to his own sacrifice on behalf of the church, implores the Christian community in Ephesus "to walk in a manner worthy of the calling to which you have been called, with all humility and gentleness, with patience, bearing with one another in love, eager to maintain the unity of the Spirit in the bond of peace" (Ephesians 4:1-3).

Loving the church sacrificially with humility, gentleness, and patience is not just for *members* of the church. It's the duty, calling, and requirement of all those who have been appointed as *leaders* within it. Pastors, overseers, and servants of the church are called to pursue reconciliation with all those who find themselves estranged, embittered, and even hostile to the church. In this way, those leading the church are called to passionately (and sacrificially) seek out the Abbys of the world with *all* humility, gentleness, and patience. It's only when the entire church, as the body of Christ, loves one another in this way that the church is able to maintain the unity of the Spirit in the bond of peace.

Finally, being the body of Christ points to Christ's *ongoing provision* for his body. Paul says, "For no one ever hated his own flesh, but *nourishes* and cherishes it, just as Christ does the church" (Ephesians 5:29, emphasis added).

Not only did Christ sacrificially give himself up (once and for all) for the church, but as our divine husband, Christ continues (present tense) to give *himself* to the church. While there are numerous ways Christ does this, the *primary* way he nourishes the church is through the Lord's Supper (also referred to as "Communion" or "Eucharist").[13]

Instead of leaving his bride with a distant (or only spiritual) memory of himself, Christ, as our Tremendous Lover, ordained (set apart) the earthly elements of bread and wine as the means by which he would *personally* and *intimately* commune with his people.[14] In doing so, Christ established *himself* as the substance of the Supper.[15] In the words of John Calvin, "Christ is the matter or (if you prefer) the substance of all the sacraments; for in him they have all their firmness, and they do not promise anything apart from him."[16]

To the evangelical ear, Calvin's words sound unorthodox (if not flat-out heretical). *How can Christ be the substance of such creaturely means as bread and wine? How is that possible?* Again, we need look no further than the Incarnation for the answer. Through the person of Christ, God united the fullness of himself with ordinary, physical means such as flesh and blood. In this way, Christ himself is the "quintessential sacrament"[17]—the ultimate example and definitive proof that God not only acts upon the physical from afar but also is really present in and through the physical means in which he chooses to act. And when the bride of Christ gathers together as the body of Christ to celebrate the body of Christ broken and the blood of Christ shed, Christ is most certainly present not just *with* them but also *within* them. In this way, the church is able both to deepen the reality of her personal and corporate union with Christ and to continually commune with the risen Christ who nurtures the church during her sojourning here on earth.

When I think about experiencing Christ in Communion this way, I can't help but think about my friend Bill.

## BILL'S STORY: THE MYSTERY OF CHRIST IN YOU

A day or two after meeting Abby, I met Bill. Unlike Abby, Bill wasn't raised in the church. In fact, he didn't come to faith in Jesus until much later in life. After going through a gut-wrenching divorce, he was invited by a coworker to a "new church" near his home in upstate New York.

"I didn't need much convincing," Bill said with a chuckle. "The first time I went, I remember being blown away with how different the church was. They played music from the radio, the pastor was young and energetic, and the people were super friendly. I had never seen anything like it. So I kept going."

After attending the church for several months, Bill said, the message "finally sunk in." Distraught from his divorce, Bill prayed to receive Christ and joined the church. But after a year, Bill's company transferred him to Charlotte. "Gosh, that was nine years ago," Bill said. "But it was the best thing that ever happened to me." As Bill continued to tell his story, I understood why.

Within the first year of his move, Bill joined a church much like the one he had left in New York, met and married his wife, and started a family. He attributed all this to the local church he joined that first year of living in Charlotte.

"That church really helped me put my life back together," Bill said. "After my wife and I married, we joined the church and were members for, well, up until last month. My faith really grew at that church. Over the years, I served on the parking team and my wife served in the children's department. Our children loved it, and we made a lot of lifelong friends. But last year, I started to 'check out' a little."

"What do you mean?" I asked.

"Well, I thought it was me at first," Bill replied, "but then I realized it wasn't. The church started to change. The services started to feel more like a concert than a church service. It was lights and lasers and all sorts of crazy things. The young kids loved it. Shoot, I did too at first. But over time, it turned into one big production.

"There was one service a few months ago," Bill continued, "where I sat back in my chair and wondered, *Is this all there is?* Something was missing; I couldn't put my finger on it."

I took a sip of coffee. "What did you do?" I asked.

"Well, I wanted to say something to my wife, but I didn't want her to think I wasn't happy there. She was basically raised in that church. But when I finally brought it up, I was surprised to find out that she had been feeling the same way.

"We stayed. Our kids loved it and we had a lot of really great friends there. So we decided to tough it out instead of uprooting the kids and church hopping."

"What seemed to be missing?" I prodded.

"Honestly, the presence of Jesus," Bill said. "The services became dry and lifeless. The pastor is a really great guy, and I loved his sermons, but we began to feel disconnected from Jesus and others in the church.

"Look," Bill continued, "I know all the right answers. I know Jesus is there through the worship, the preaching, and the people, but I rarely sensed the Holy Spirit during the services. So instead of us leaving the church, the Lord moved us across town."

After Bill's wife accepted a job closer to the city, they sold their home in South Charlotte and moved into a rental home in a well-known neighborhood. That's where, Bill said, they "stumbled on" their new church.

"One Sunday morning I went for a walk, and I noticed a little white church on a hill about a half mile from our house. There were families from the neighborhood walking to church, kids were playing in the yard, it seemed like a big family. So we decided to check it out."

"Did you?"

"Yeah," Bill responded, almost cutting me off in his excitement. "It was way more traditional than we were used to. But it was a nice change. It was *just* boring enough for me to settle down and connect with God."

Then Bill's voice turned more serious. "Towards the end of that first service, the pastor held up a loaf of bread and a cup of juice and talked about the meaning of Communion. He said Communion was one of the ways they celebrated the presence of Jesus not only with them, but in them each week. I had *never* heard that before," Bill confessed. "But when the pastor said it, I was like, 'That's it!' Yeah! Jesus *in* me, the hope of glory."

I smiled and nodded, surprised by Bill's memorization of Scripture. "What happened?"

"Jesus met me! What do you think?" Bill said, excited as ever. "I didn't know if we should go up or not, but the pastor was adamant that Communion wasn't just for members of their church, but for anyone who believed in Jesus. So I went.

"Standing in line to receive Communion was really neat," Bill continued. "It reminded me that we are all in need of Jesus. It was like one big public confession that we are all broken, busted-up sinners in need of God's grace.

"As the pastor placed the broken piece of bread in my hand and offered the cup for me to dip it in, I thought about Jesus and all he went through," Bill continued. "As I ate it, I imagined Jesus in me. I pictured Jesus being a part of me, like the bread and the juice. I had never imagined Christ's presence meeting me in Communion like that. It was one of the most surreal things I had ever experienced in church.

"Now," Bill continued, "I can't wait to go to church. We

walk to church as a family and walk back talking about what the kids learned in Sunday school. It's great. And most weeks, after the sermon, we take Communion. And every single time, Jesus meets me in a real and deep way."

Bill and his family went on to join the "little white church on the hill." As he continued to share, I thought about Abby. I thought how cool it would be if she could hear Bill's story. I wondered if maybe the "substance" Abby was looking for might be the "substance" Calvin spoke about and the substance Bill experiences most weeks at that little church.

"I now know I'm a part of Christ's body," Bill said. "I wish everyone could feel like that."

## DISCUSSION QUESTIONS

1. *What has been your experience with the church? Does Abby's story resonate with you? Explain.*
2. *Complete this sentence: "Being united to Christ, and an individual member of his body, makes me feel _____." Explain your answer.*
3. *What is your current view of the Lord's Supper? Did Bill's story resonate with you? Explain.*

# 10

# THE MISSION OF CHRIST: SO THAT THE WORLD MAY KNOW

*The glory that you have given me I have given to them, that they*
*may be one even as we are one, I in them and you in me.*

JESUS (JOHN 17:22-23)

IN OUR LITTLE COUNTRY CHURCH in East Tennessee where I
grew up, there was a dark blue banner in the choir loft with
the words "Go Therefore" written in a glittering gold. Every
Sunday, the simple message on the banner reminded me of
the mission of the church and my responsibility to "go therefore and make disciples of all nations, baptizing them in the
name of the Father and of the Son and of the Holy Spirit,
teaching them to observe all that I have commanded you"
(Matthew 28:19-20).

This "great commission" of Jesus inspired and terrified
me as a child. It inspired me because I wanted the world to
experience Jesus as I had. But it terrified me that Jesus might

send me to some remote village in Africa (or across the street) to do so!

While I loved Jesus, "sharing my faith" scared the daylights out of me. Try going door to door "witnessing" to people about Jesus with Tourette's! I'll spare you the details, but it's funny. Hilarious even. I have an entire stand-up comedy routine in my mind, ready to go at a moment's notice.

The first time I went out "witnessing," I felt like I was selling cheesecakes or candy bars. Except the motivation wasn't to win the red hard hat with the cup holders on the side—it was to "win souls" to heaven. And as a disciple, I was called to "go" and "tell" as many people as possible about Jesus. Truth be known, most days I would have much rather sold cheesecakes. But cheesecakes don't get you into heaven.

Sometimes I wonder how the disciples must have felt the first time they heard Jesus say, "Go and make disciples of all nations." Were they inspired—chomping at the bit to get out into the world and tell people about Jesus? Or were they terrified and confused, short-circuited by the enormity of the task? How *exactly* were they to go into *all* the world and make disciples of *all* nations? They didn't own a car. Planes weren't invented yet. They didn't even know what a bicycle was. The only thing they had were their own two feet wrapped in leather.

And how were they to remember everything Jesus had commanded them in order to teach others? The poor guys had trouble staying awake around Jesus, much less memorizing what he had to say.

And if, somehow, the disciples were able to fulfill Jesus'

command, then what? *So* what? You would think that Jesus would have given them a little more insight as to how (and why) they were to go.

As we have already seen, Jesus gave his disciples much of what they needed to know in his farewell speech (John 13–16). Jesus specifically instructed them to wait for the Holy Spirit and said that the Spirit would dwell in them in order to help them. Also, the Holy Spirit would somehow make the disciples "one" with Jesus, allowing them to share in the love between him and his Father. It would also be the Holy Spirit who would teach them and bring everything Jesus had taught to their minds.

But what if the greatest insight concerning the "how" and the "why" of the great commission isn't something Jesus taught in John 13–16 but rather something Jesus prayed for in John 17? What if making disciples of all nations boiled down not to a farewell address but to one simple yet profound phrase: "may be"?

## "MAY BE"

According to John's Gospel, after Jesus concluded his goodbye speech, he "lifted up his eyes to heaven" to pray (John 17:1). It's not clear whether his disciples heard Jesus' prayer. Maybe he sent them on their way and found a quiet spot by himself. Maybe Jesus prayed right in front of them. We don't know. But we do know that John, the disciple Jesus loved,[1] recorded every word. Who knows, maybe John snuck in close to Jesus without him noticing (if that's possible!). Maybe the Holy Spirit brought Jesus' words to John's mind through divine inspiration. Again, we aren't sure. But what we are sure of is what (and for whom) Jesus prayed. And embedded within Jesus' prayer is one of the most important things the disciples needed to know concerning how and why to fulfill great commission.

> Holy Father, protect them [the disciples] by the power of your name—the name you gave me—so that *they may be one* as we are one. . . .
> I pray also for those who will believe in me through their message, that *all of them may be one*, Father, just as you are in me and I am in you. . . .
> I have given them the glory that you gave me, that *they may be one* as we are one: I in them and you in me. *May they be brought to complete unity to let the world know that you sent me and have loved them even as you have loved me.*
> JOHN 17:11, 20-23, NIV, EMPHASIS ADDED

In his prayer, Jesus clarifies the great commission for the disciples (and us). How were the disciples to "Go into all the world and proclaim the gospel to the whole creation" (Mark 16:15)? How were they to baptize new converts and teach them to obey everything Jesus commanded?

*As one.*

Three times Jesus prays that his disciples may be one just as he and the Father are one. The first time, Jesus prays for the twelve (minus Judas). Then he prays that *all those who believe* in him through their message (that's you and me) may be one. The third time, Jesus seems to pray that his disciples may be one *along with* everyone who believes in Christ through their message. Each time Jesus qualifies "oneness" as being united to the familial bond between the Father and the Son.

Upon his plea for believers to be one, Jesus sets forth his most awe-inspiring vision for the mission of the church: that all believers everywhere "may . . . be brought to complete unity to let the world know that you [the Father] sent me [the Son] and have loved them even as you have loved me" (John 17:23, NIV).

Over the years, I have come to see these words as a *plea* with a *promise*. The plea—for complete unity. The promise: that the world will know *two* things.

First, the Son *really was* sent of the Father. Visible unity among believers proves the truth of the Incarnation. Just as the Father revealed himself to the world through Christ, the church, as the body of Christ, manifests the truth of the Incarnation to the world. "Whoever has seen me," Jesus said, "has seen the Father" (John 14:9). As the Word made flesh, Jesus embodied the very nature of God for the world to see. In the same way, the church, as the body of Christ, makes visible the nature of Jesus Christ to the world.

Several years ago now, the Barna Group conducted a national study of how Christians and non-Christians viewed Christianity and the church. Based on the responses of thousands of young adults, ages sixteen to twenty-nine, Christianity was mainly described as being homophobic, judgmental, hypocritical, insensitive, intolerant, and too focused on getting people "saved."[2] While these characteristics do not describe all Christians (or churches), unfortunately the study proved what many Christians feared: The church has an image problem. But the problem is much deeper than just the church's image. If the church represents Christ on earth, *Jesus himself* has an image problem. The study proved a sobering reality: The world determines who Jesus is based on how the church portrays him.

But what if the church united around what we are for, instead of what we are against? How would the world perceive Jesus then? What if the church stood in visible unity and full communion with each other despite our differences? What if the church united around the truth of our union with Christ and proclaimed to the world with one voice that "God did not send his Son into the world to condemn the world, but to save the world through him" (John 3:17, NIV)? What would the world believe about Jesus through that kind of church? (We'll get to that in just a minute.)

Second, Jesus promised that the world will know that the Father *really does* love them as much as his very own Son. Unity among believers not only shows forth the truth of the Incarnation, but it proves the truth (and depth) of God's love. Just as the Father revealed the fullness of his love through Christ, the entire body of Christ—the church—reveals the truth of the Father's love to the world.

This love is manifested through the whole church loving and serving each other primarily, and secondly our neighbor—any and every human being, but especially the poor, the widow, and the orphan.[3] The Father's love is also realized through the proclamation of the Good News by the church to all those imprisoned by sin—shackled by guilt, fear, and self-hatred (see Luke 4:16-20).

According to Jesus, visible unity among Christians is the single greatest apologetic that proves he was sent of the Father and the Father loves the world as much as his own Son. Conversely, though, visible *disunity* among Christians is the number one apologetic that discredits the Christian faith. Sandra Toenies Keating, professor of theology at Providence College and leading expert in Muslim-Christian dialogue, agrees. During her plenary session at the 2015 National Workshop on Christian Unity, Dr. Keating stunned the crowd, stating, "The visible division among Christians has served as the long-standing apologetic of the Islamic faith to discount the truth of Christianity."[4]

Her statement silenced the room. It reminded me of Mike, a young man I met during my week of meetings. Mike was raised in a Christian home but became an agnostic in high school, shortly after his parents divorced. For Mike, it wasn't doctrine that undermined the legitimacy of Christianity, it was the visible disunion and lack of charity among Christians. For an hour he argued that the division among Christians "discredits the message of Jesus."

As Mike shared, I couldn't help but think about what my father told me when Monica and I started having kids. He said the number one way children know whether or not the are loved is when "mom and dad love each other." I have never forgotten those words. Anyone who has experienced family division, discord, or divorce will tell you that the children are the ones who take the biggest hit. And from my experience, the primary burden many Millennials (those born after 1981) have concerning Christianity is the disunity they see in the church and the lack of love among Christians. I have found that observing such disunity somehow mirrors the frightening division they sense in their own soul and confirms what they fear most—that they are alone in an unloving world.

What if Christians loved and cared for each other *just as* the Father loves and cares for his *own* Son? What would the world think then? What if the church, in a world full of division, stood unified as visible (and tangible) proof of God's love? What impact would that kind of church have on our cities, our nation, and our world? What impact would that kind of church have on Mike?

I'm convinced that when Christians (of all denominations and traditions) awaken to and live out our common union with Christ and each other, the church of Jesus Christ will be the most beautiful, majestic, and irresistible force on the planet. But what would such a church look like? How might believers begin to love and serve one another, and work together instead of apart? Let me tell you a story.

## WE ARE ONE: THE CHARLOTTE/ONE STORY
It all started with one simple question. Well, it actually started in the back of theology class.

I was in my final semester as an MDiv student. When I wasn't studying a bunch of "ologies," I served as the twenty-something pastor at a megachurch in the northern part of town. (I'm from the South; I still refer to cities as "towns." Don't judge me.) I loved seminary, but I loved my job even more. I know some have had not-so-great experiences in large churches, but I loved it. Although I was an inexperienced, naive country boy from East Tennessee, the pastor allowed me to sit on committees and preach from the main stage on the weekends. He gave me a ton of freedom to fail. And fail I did. (One failure, creatively dubbed "my first sermon at the church," dominated the church blooper reel at the staff Christmas party that year. But that's another story.)

After running the twentysomething ministry into the ground, I licked my wounds and relaunched the ministry under a new name: NeXus. (No, not the hair product. That's spelled with two x's.) I was convinced that NeXus would redeem my failure and be the twentysomething savior of Charlotte, reaching thousands of young professionals (that's urban talk for "young adults") and transforming the city for Christ.

Not only did NeXus have a slick one-word name (as most twentysomething ministries do), we offered small groups, social groups, and service opportunities. But the real "nexus" of the ministry was our Thursday night worship service. We brought in the best worship leaders from around the city. Our messages were conversational and geared toward the lives of twentysomethings living in the area. We had lights, cameras, and all the Starbucks action you could want.

After a year (I'll spare you the gory details) we started wondering if NeXus should be niXed. Worship services rarely topped forty in attendance. Small groups divided and dwindled. Social events were awkward and, well, awkward. No matter what we tried, or how we tried it, reaching the twentysomethings of the city proved to be much more difficult than I imagined.

I began to question myself as a pastor and my calling to young adult ministry. I was beyond discouraged. *Demolished* would be a better word. The worst part was I had no one (except my wife) to share my frustrations and insecurities. You just can't go around the church office mumbling in a low voice, "I'm a failure. I shouldn't be in ministry. I'm fooling myself."

Desperate, I began to pray for God to send me someone I could talk to—someone in ministry I could learn from, who would share the heavy burden of ministering to twentysomethings in the city.

## WHAT? YOU TOO?

Because Gordon-Conwell is an interdenominational seminary, classes are peppered with church leaders from different denominations. Most of the time, people kept to themselves. I did too. The crushing weight of family, ministry, and seminary is enough to make anyone crawl into their shell. But I was extroverted and *just* desperate enough to reach out to some fellow classmates regarding my ministry disaster.

One night during theology class, I noticed a group of

young guys sitting in the back of the room. It could have been their age, but something about them suggested they might know a thing or two about twentysomethings. When class dismissed for break, instead of going to get coffee with everyone else, I quickly gathered my notes against my chest, scurried to the back of the room, and quickly set up right beside the cluster of five chairs. When the group returned from break (Starbucks in tow), there I was, sitting cool and collected, legs crossed—working on my computer as if nothing was out of order.

After a quick round of introductions, my intuition was confirmed: They all were involved (in some capacity) in twentysomething ministry! But that's not all—each was on staff at a local church in the city. I couldn't believe it. God didn't give me one person to talk to; he gave me five. It was a miracle. But what happened next was even more miraculous.

As I shared the difficulties I was experiencing reaching twentysomethings, each one told an eerily similar story back to the group. Regardless of the size or denomination of the churches represented, we each shared the *exact* same dilemma: Twentysomethings were not interested in our efforts.

That night in the back of theology class, I made five new (and now lifelong) friends. Our friendship formed the way C. S. Lewis described—when one person looked at the other and said, "What? You too? I thought I was the only one . . ."[5]

To my surprise, the five were merely acquaintances before that night. And none had shared their personal struggles in ministry with each other. But after looking one another in the eye and exclaiming, "What? You too?" a relationship began—one that would change twentysomething ministry in Charlotte for the next ten years (and counting!).

## OUT OF THE MANY, ONE

While we didn't realize it at the time, the interdenominational friendship the six of us developed was unusual for pastors in Charlotte at the time. In 2005, the spiritual climate in Charlotte wasn't the most healthy. In fact, it had reached a tipping point.

Charlotte is known as a "city of churches." Close to one thousand Christian communities blanket our landscape. Soaring steeples and swaying flags signal the presence of the church on almost every corner. But more churches does not necessarily equal better Christianity.

Few pastors met with or even communicated with one another. New church plants (at one point I was told eleven per month) would "parachute" into the city with wonderful intentions of "reaching the city for Christ." But instead of reaching the city, the influx of so many new churches seemed to only reinforce the individualized perception each church had of the other. Christians of different denominations, races, and traditions were suspicious of one another and the "agenda" each church had for the city. In many ways, the churches of Charlotte in 2005 reflected what Paul observed the church in Corinth to be: divided. Paul writes:

> For it has been reported to me by Chloe's people
> that there is quarreling among you. . . . What I mean
> is that each one of you says, "I follow Paul," or "I
> follow Apollos," or "I follow Cephas," or "I follow
> Christ." Is Christ divided? Was Paul crucified for
> you? Or were you baptized in the name of Paul?[6]

I CORINTHIANS 1:11-13

While it would be unfair to say that *all* churches (or Christians) in Charlotte contributed to our disunity, it is fair to say that few, if any, were doing anything about it. The reason is understandable. Most pastors I know deeply care about church unity but find it impossible to address, much less to solve. Pastors and church leaders, buried by the weight of caring for and leading their own communities, simply do not have the time or emotional energy to think about Christian unity. I know. I was one of them!

Against this dark backdrop of disunity, though, God placed a glimmering speck of hope within the hearts of six twentysomething pastors. Over the semester, our friendship grew into a relationship. Before long, our relationship morphed into trust. After a year, our trust gave way to profound love for one another. And it was out of our love for each other that one simple question emerged: *Do you think we could reach twentysomethings better together than apart?*

The question pierced our hearts and brought our souls to a hush. In one regard, we all knew the question was coming; we were convinced God would one day make visible our love for one another. We just didn't know how, when, or where. Each of us had been involved in citywide events in the past that had tanked, causing us to grimace a little at the question. But the difference this time was that the question wasn't emotional or merely anecdotal but deeply theological: *If Christ is not divided, and we are a part of Christ, then we are not divided either.*

We sat silent—staring one another in the eyes as we had almost a year earlier. But instead of feeling excited, we felt anxious and afraid—anticipating the next logical question. I broke the silence and asked the inevitable: "Do you think our pastors will let us?" None of us could answer the question.

Before running right to our pastors and asking their blessing, we committed to pray together—asking God that he would open up a door for us to walk through.

⁀

Instead of a door flying open, I received a phone call from one of my professors and mentors at Gordon-Conwell. He was serving on staff at a local church just south of the city.

"Dave," he said, his voice laced with excitement, "several of us pastors in the south part of Charlotte have been meeting for the last few months praying about doing a multi-church outreach service geared toward twentysomethings. I just thought of you. Would you like to be a part of the conversation?"

I nearly dropped the phone. I shook with excitement as I explained what God had been doing in my heart and the hearts of my new friends. We scheduled a meeting for us all to meet, talk, and pray.

When both groups got together, it felt like a family reunion. Although we didn't know each other, we all shared the same passion to see God work in love and unity in our city. One of the pastors stood up and read from John 17—the same passage our group of six had prayed over for a year.

"Charlotte is one of the fastest-growing cities in America for twenty- and thirtysomethings," the pastor continued. "Many of them do not know Christ. And the problem is too big for any one church in the city to solve. We need to respond as the church, represent Christ to them, and reintroduce them to what the church really is—one body."

Questions mounted—intelligent questions, practical questions, theological questions. "What about our different views of the atonement? What about the gifts of the Spirit? How will this new effort fit into the overall life and mission of the local church?" While we didn't have all the answers right away, it was clear God was calling us to make visible the love that had been forged among us.

After several months of conversation and prayer, the two groups became one in love and mission. And when our group of six approached our pastors with what God was doing, each gave their blessing. God was on the move (as he always is).

—

"Charlotte/ONE. Let's call it Charlotte/ONE," my mentor said during one particular meeting. "Jesus prayed that we would be one, so let's show the twentysomethings of our city that the church in Charlotte is one."

We all agreed on the name (relieved that it had more than two syllables). We also agreed to share the work required to launch Charlotte/ONE. Each of us was serving on staff at a church and didn't have the bandwidth (or desire) to oversee a multichurch outreach service. I certainly didn't want to. I couldn't even lead the twentysomething ministry at one church, much less one that belonged to multiple churches.

But when it came time to appoint a spokesperson, all fingers pointed to me. I was humbled by their confidence in me to communicate the heart of what God was doing among us. Despite my own doubts and insecurities, I accepted.

On the first Tuesday in May 2006, Charlotte/ONE became a reality. A local church in the city donated their gymnasium to host the gatherings. But there was a catch—we could only have Charlotte/ONE there for the first month. After four weeks, we'd have to find another venue. We saw this as an opportunity to beta test our vision. If twentysomethings responded, we'd continue. If not, we would be thankful for the four weeks we were able to platform our love for one another. Either way, Charlotte/ONE was already a success.

That Tuesday, we set out chairs for one hundred people—that would have doubled if not tripled any one of our individual twentysomething ministries. When the gym doors flung open, over two hundred people walked in. We couldn't believe our eyes.

"Where did all these twentysomethings come from?" I asked one of the pastors.

Staring in disbelief himself, he replied, "I have no idea."

I walked onstage to welcome the crowd and was taken by what God appeared to be doing. After telling everyone where the bathrooms were and inviting them to "say hello to their neighbor," I turned to John 17 and began to read. I talked about the love that had developed between us as pastors, and how our love for one another led us to publicly demonstrate our unity as Christians.

"So, as *one*," I said in conclusion, "our desire is not just to talk about Jesus' love. We are here to show you how much Jesus and the church in our city love *you*."

Applause echoed off the walls of the gymnasium. I tried to interject, but the applause kept building—growing louder and louder. I stood back from the microphone and joined the celebration. For close to two minutes (a long time if you are clapping) the twentysomethings in that gymnasium cheered, whistled, and applauded the vision of John 17. I stood, observing the celebration, and wondered if unity and collaboration among Christians might be the next reformation in the church.

When the four-week "trial" came to a close, it was clear

that God had opened a door. Over those four weeks, we had seen multiple people come to faith in Christ and reconnect with local churches, and on the last night, over four hundred twentysomethings crammed into the gym to celebrate Jesus and Christian unity. After the last service, a young guy stopped me as I was walking to my car. He asked me to share a bit more about the mission and vision of Charlotte/ONE. I stumbled over myself and the vision for five minutes trying to explain.

"Okay, okay. Gotcha," the young man said, cutting me off. "I'd like to continue talking. I'm interested in being more a part of what you guys are doing. Would you be willing to grab dinner one night this week to discuss?"

"You bet," I said.

Over a really nice prime rib, the young man shared how he and his friends had been praying for churches in Charlotte to offer something like Charlotte/ONE. "And to support your work," he said with a twinkle in his eye, "we'd like to commit to a financial gift. How does $100,000 sound?"

My Tourette's nearly went through the roof! A hundred thousand dollars? *How does a twentysomething have $100,000?* I didn't know how to respond. What do you say? "Cool, man, thanks"?

I shook his hand and cried a few tears. I called my mentor on the way home and explained what had happened. His response still rings in my ear to this day: "Well, God is honoring the final prayer of his Son. If I had $100,000 to give to my son's dying wish, I'd do the same."

Equipped (and now responsible) for both four hundred people and $100,000, the leadership team gathered to pray about how best to continue. The pastors involved with Charlotte/ONE had been around the block a few times; they didn't want attendance or money to be the deciding factor as to whether or not we should keep going. So we took the rest of the summer to pray, and then the pastors gathered back together in August with their decision.

"We feel we should continue," my mentor said, on behalf of the pastors. "But we need a leader. Dave, we want you to be the director of Charlotte/ONE."

I didn't need to even pray about it. I had been praying for Charlotte/ONE and my role in it for over a year. I finished seminary, stepped down from my position at the church I loved, and began to love and serve the local church of Charlotte.

—

Ten years later, Charlotte/ONE has grown to be one of the largest outreaches to twentysomethings in the southeastern United States. Over forty local churches now call Charlotte/ONE "theirs." And it is. Charlotte/ONE is not an outreach service of one individual church inviting other churches to be a part of what they are doing. Instead, Charlotte/ONE is a unified effort of *many* local churches who together reflect the *one* church of Charlotte. And the results have been staggering. At a recent CharlotteONE gathering, close to four hundred young adults participated in a survey to help gauge the effectiveness of our efforts over the years.

> 42 percent had connected or reconnected to a local church.
> 31 percent had made decisions for Christ.
> 57 percent had connected to a local nonprofit.
> 98 percent grew in their understanding of Christ.
> 91 percent felt more comfortable living in Charlotte.
> 90 percent had made a good friend.

In addition, 78 percent decided to remain in Charlotte because of CharlotteONE. The first statistic caught the attention of churches in the city; the last statistic landed me in a meeting with city officials, who thanked us for helping them reach and retain young professionals.

Over the years, CharlotteONE has influenced other local churches in cities across the nation to begin similar unified efforts to reach twentysomethings together. One such city is Phoenix, Arizona. In 2011, local churches in "the Valley" banded together to launch Phoenix/ONE and invited me to speak at their kickoff event at Historic First Presbyterian Church, a few blocks away from Chase Field. Over four hundred twentysomethings gathered that night. I spoke about our union with Christ and Jesus' prayer in John 17 for the church to be who she already is in him—*one*. I told the Charlotte/ONE story and encouraged them to write their own story of love and unity. Four years later, Phoenix/ONE grew to over a thousand young adults, seeing the same level of local church connections and impact in the city.

Since then, I've had the privilege of sharing the Charlotte/ONE story with church leaders in Austin, Texas; Denver, Colorado; Chicago, Illinois; Indianapolis, Indiana; and Atlanta, Georgia. God, in his grace, took the love five people had for me (and I for them) and has grown it to include hundreds of dear friends across the nation who are committed to seeing the church love and move together as one. And it all started when a few people looked at each other and said, "What? You too?"

## GO THEREFORE

While the CharlotteONE story is motivating, don't let it mislead you. You don't have to be in vocational ministry or seminary to love others—that's *every* Christian's duty and privilege. You don't have to be a pastor or on staff at a church to pray and work for visible unity among believers in your city. Again, that's what *all of us* are called to do.

But in order to see unity among believers, we first have to awaken to our union with Christ. For our union with one another is not something we *pursue*, it's *someone* we are *united to*—the living, breathing person of Jesus Christ. He's not an ethereal figure; he's a real person. You and I are united to the same Jesus who said to Thomas, "Put your finger here, and see my hands; and put out your hand, and place it in my side" (John 20:27).

Our union with Christ is not just "the central truth of

the whole doctrine of salvation," as John Murray said.[7] Our union with Christ is the central truth (and foundational reality) of our union with each other. For if *the best* you and I can hope for today is to have a "close relationship" with Jesus, then inevitably *the most* you and I can try to achieve with each other is a "close relationship" as well. But in awakening to our union with the person of Christ (who is *not* divided), the church (regardless of her division) can begin to unite around common-union of who we *already are* in Christ Jesus—perfectly one with each other.

"Therefore, go," Jesus says. Go to your job and allow your coworkers to see Christ. Go to your school and image the risen Christ to your classmates. Go into your churches and be the body of Christ. Go into the world, Jesus says, and "love one another: just as I have loved you" (John 13:34). This is Christ's command to you and to me. How are we to fulfill such an impossible command?

The answer might be closer than you think.

## DISCUSSION QUESTIONS

1. *When you think about "going into all the world and making disciples," how do you feel? Explain.*
2. *The author argues that all those united to Christ are already one with each other. How would this change your understanding of (and participation in) Christian unity in your city?*
3. *Read John 17:20-23. How is the Holy Spirit working in your city to bring about visible unity among Christians?*

# NOTES

**A WORD BEFORE**

1. Philip Yancey, *The Jesus I Never Knew* (Grand Rapids, MI: Zondervan, 1995).

**INTRODUCTION: THE WHITE ARROW**

1. Karissa Giuliano, "13 Famous Logos with Hidden Messages," May 1, 2015, accessed October 21, 2015, http://www.cnbc.com/2015/05/01/13 -famous-logos-that-require-a-double-take.html.
2. Brennan Manning, *The Furious Longing of God* (Colorado Springs: David C. Cook, 2009), 30. Capitalization in the original, per Brennan's fiery spirit.
3. John Murray, *Redemption Accomplished and Applied* (Grand Rapids: Eerdmans, 1955), 161. Emphasis added.
4. John Calvin, *Institutes of the Christian Religion*, 3.2, ed. John T. McNeill, trans. Ford Lewis Battles, Library of Christian Classics, vols. 20–21 (Philadelphia: Westminster, 1960), 570. Emphasis added.
5. Jean Vanier, *Drawn into the Mystery of Jesus through the Gospel of John* (New York: Paulist, 2004), 296.
6. Brennan Manning, *The Ragamuffin Gospel* (Sisters, OR: Multnomah, 1990), 69.

**CHAPTER 2: THE BOND OF BREATH**

1. Oxford English Dictionary, 3rd ed., s.v. "ineffable."

**CHAPTER 3: THE MYSTERY OF GOD**

1. "God *himself*" is typically understood to denote the entire Trinity of God (Father, Son, and Holy Spirit). However, throughout the Scriptures "God"

*typically* refers to the Father—the first person of the Trinity. For this reason, the phrase "God himself" is most rightly understood to refer to "*the Father* himself." But for the sake of familiarity (and the fact that "God themselves" sounds suspect), I have chosen to retain the phrase "God himself" to denote the Father, Son, and Spirit.

2. Emphasis added. For additional Scriptures showing the singular plurality of God, see Genesis 3:22; Isaiah 48:16; Matthew 3:16-17; 28:19; 2 Corinthians 13:14.

3. Michael Reeves, in his book *Delighting in the Trinity*, makes the case that if God's primary identity is that of "Creator" or "Ruler," then creation was *necessary* in order for God to "be who he is." In this way, according to Reeves, "God turns out to be pitifully weak: he *needs* us." Conversely, if God's primary identity is that of "Father," then God's identity is not dependent upon creating or ruling over creation but in being a Father to a real and distinct Son. Therefore, Reeves concludes, God is first and foremost a Father who "finds his very identity, his Fatherhood, in loving and giving out his life and being to the Son." See Michael Reeves, *Delighting in the Trinity: An Introduction to the Christian Faith* (Downers Grove, IL: InterVarsity, 2012), 19–21, 27.

4. See, for example, John 3:16; 5:25; 10:36; 11:4; 15:9; 17:1, 23-26; 20:31.

5. See Matthew 3:13-17; 17:1-13.

6. "Revelation" in Latin is *revelatio*, meaning "to pull back the curtain."

7. "Spirit" in Greek (*pneuma*) can also be translated "breath."

## CHAPTER 4: FAMOUS LAST WORDS

1. Jim Valvano, "Espy Award Speech," March 4, 1993, accessed October 21, 2015, at http://www.jimmyv.org/about-us/remembering-jim/jimmy-v-espy-awards-speech/.

2. "Full extent of his love" is the NIV 1984 rendering of John 13:1.

3. Donald Fairbairn, *Life in the Trinity: An Introduction to Theology with the Help of the Church Fathers* (Downers Grove, IL: InterVarsity, 2009), 193, emphasis added.

4. The phrases "by grace" and "by nature," in relation to the disciples' union with Christ and Christ's union with the Father, are an important distinction made by early church fathers such as Cyril of Alexandria and Athanasius. Donald Fairbairn, commenting on the writings of both, states, "The Word, Jesus Christ, is the one, true, natural Son of God, who is one of the persons of the Trinity, equal to (and in terms of attributes, even identical to) the Father. He [Christ] is the only one who has eternally been in a filial relationship with God the Father. In contrast, those who believe

in Christ are sons and daughters by adoption, by grace. . . . Thus, in the writings of the early church, the phrases 'by nature' and 'by grace' clearly distinguish Christ/the Word/the Son from those who are born of God by believing in the Son." See Fairbairn, *Life in the Trinity*, 134–135.

5. At this point, some may be asking, "What about the Spirit? Doesn't the Holy Spirit share in the love between the Father and the Son as well?" Certainly. But while sharing in the same relationship of love and fellowship, the Spirit is not in a *familial* relation to the Father the way the Son is. Again, Donald Fairbairn helps clarify: "Even though the persons [of the Trinity] are identical in terms of characteristics, they are not identical in the way they are related to one another. The Son is begotten by the Father, and the Spirit proceeds from the Father (and perhaps also from the Son as well). . . . In other words, he [the Spirit] is not in a filial relation to the Father, the way the Son is, but rather he is in a processional relation; he goes out ('proceeds') from the Father to accomplish his will." Therefore, the role of the Holy Spirit within the Trinity of God is not to exemplify the Son's relation to the Father; the Son himself does that. Instead, the Holy Spirit (while perfectly one with the Father and the Son) draws our attention (and draws us into) the familial love between the Father and the Son (but common to the Spirit as well). See Fairbairn, *Life in the Trinity*, 52–58.

6. Brennan Manning, *The Furious Longing of God* (Colorado Springs: David C. Cook, 2009), 59.

7. Robert Letham, *Union with Christ: In Scripture, History, and Theology* (Phillipsburg, NJ: P&R Publishing, 2011), 137.

## CHAPTER 5: UNION TO DISUNION

1. C. S. Lewis, *Mere Christianity* (San Francisco: HarperOne, 2009), 175.

2. Certainly, the union of the Father, Son, and Spirit is not merely relational, but one of substance and essence, as the Nicene Creed affirms.

3. M. Douglas Meeks, "The Social Trinity and Property," in *God's Life in Trinity*, ed. Miroslav Volf and Michael Welker (Minneapolis: Augsburg Fortress, 2006), 15.

4. Gerald Bray, *The Doctrine of God* (Downers Grove, IL: InterVarsity, 1993), 158.

5. Dom Eugene Boylan, *This Tremendous Lover* (Charlotte, NC: TAN Books, 2013), 4.

6. I snagged this phraseology from George A. Maloney, *The Spirit Broods over the World* (Staten Island, NY: Alba House, 1993), especially chapters 1 and 3.

7. Michael Reeves, *Delighting in the Trinity: An Introduction to the Christian Faith* (Downers Grove, IL: InterVarsity, 2012), 29.

8. In the vein of Karl Rahner, if this were not so, God would only be the giver of life, and not life itself. See Karl Rahner, *The Trinity* (New York: Herder & Herder, 1969), 101. While some scholars suggest that God breathed a "soul" into Adam (per Augustine), other theologians (such as Cyril of Alexandria) believe God breathed the Holy Spirit into the man. Donald Fairbairn, commenting on Cyril of Alexandria as well as other church fathers, states, "God gave Adam the Holy Spirit himself, thus linking him to the Son in whose image he was created and causing him [Adam] to share in the fellowship of the Trinity." See Donald Fairbairn, *Life in the Trinity: An Introduction to Theology with the Help of the Church Fathers* (Downers Grove, IL: InterVarsity, 2009), 62–64.

9. Interestingly, the Hebrew word for "one," used to describe Adam and Eve's union in Genesis 2:24, is the same word used to denote the singularity of God in the *Shema* found in Deuteronomy 6:4: "Hear, O Israel: The LORD our God, the LORD is one." This not only seems to prove the composite unity found within Israel's God but also shows how completely and perfectly "one" Adam and Eve were!

10. Meredith G. Kline, *Kingdom Prologue* (Eugene, OR: Wipf & Stock, 2006), 80.

11. Fairbairn, *Life in the Trinity*, 98.

12. Isaiah 54:5-8; Jeremiah 3:20; 31:31-33; Ezekiel 16:32-34.

**CHAPTER 6: REUNION TO PERFECT UNION**

1. Gerard Manley Hopkins, "The Blessed Virgin Compared to the Air We Breathe" (1918), lines 17–23.

2. As a clarifying example, Nestorius believed that God the Word/Son only "filled" Jesus, similar to the way the Holy Spirit "fills" believers today. Just as a believer, though filled with the Holy Spirit, is not God the Spirit, Nestorius believed that Jesus ("filled by the Word") was not the eternal Word himself.

3. Gregory of Nazianzus, "Epistola 101," *Patrologia Graeca* 31:181c.

4. The Christology affirmed at both Ephesus and Chalcedon can be rightly attributed to Cyril of Alexandria. His theology lies behind the council's pronouncements regarding the nature of Christ.

5. For an excellent contemporary work that clearly shows how Christ himself is salvation, justification, sanctification, etc., from an evangelical perspective, see Marcus Peter Johnson, *One with Christ: An Evangelical Theology of Salvation* (Wheaton, IL: Crossway, 2013).

6. John Calvin, *Institutes of the Christian Religion* 3.2, ed. John T. McNeill, trans. Ford Lewis Battles, Library of Christian Classics, vols. 20–21 (Philadelphia: Westminster, 1960), 570. Emphasis added.

7. Robert Letham, *Union with Christ: In Scripture, History, and Theology* (Phillipsburg, NJ: P&R Publishing, 2011), 98.
8. This number also includes the phrases "in Christ Jesus," "in the Lord," and "in him."
9. For the record, while I do have both motor and vocal tics, I do not cuss unless it's on purpose.
10. I have yet to acquire a PhD. My friends who have it tell me it is a mental disorder as well. Maybe one day.
11. Quote from Kuyper's inaugural address at the dedication of the Free University. Found in *Abraham Kuyper: A Centennial Reader*, ed. James D. Bratt (Grand Rapids, MI: Eerdmans, 1998), 488.
12. See Letham, *Union with Christ*, 135.
13. The word *perfect* in the original is *epiteleo*, meaning "to finish, complete, or perfect." It's interesting to note that *epiteleo* appears in the future active tense in Philippians 1:6, denoting an action accomplished by the subject of the verb (to wit, "He [God]") that will take place in the future.
14. According to Pope John Paul II, "The entire world of men, the entire history of humanity, finds in Him [Christ] its expression before God." See John Paul II, *Crossing the Threshold of Hope* (New York: Knopf, 1994), 43.
15. In baptism, believers show forth and participate in these wonderful realities. Since Christ represented all of humanity in his person, when he was baptized two thousand years ago, he took all of humanity down with him in the baptismal waters. In the same way, when Christ rose again, he brought the promise and guarantee of new life to all. See Romans 6:4.

## CHAPTER 7: PERSONAL IDENTITY: THE MOST LOVED

1. J. I. Packer, *Knowing God* (Downers Grove, IL: InterVarsity, 1973), 206. Emphasis in the original.
2. George MacDonald, quoted in John Eldredge, *Fathered by God* (Nashville: Thomas Nelson, 2009), 29.
3. Marcus Peter Johnson, in his book *One with Christ*, quotes J. I. Packer in his lament that "the truth of adoption has been little regarded in Christian history. Apart from two last-century books, now scarcely known . . . there is no evangelical writing on it, nor has there been at any time since the Reformation, any more than there was before" (Packer, *Knowing God*, 206–207). Johnson, however, is correct in stating that many evangelicals are now correcting this omission, including Trevor Burke, *Adopted into God's Family: Exploring a Pauline Metaphor* (Downers Grove, IL: InterVarsity, 2006), and Robert A. Peterson, *Adopted by God: From Wayward Sinners to Cherished Children* (Phillipsburg, NJ: P&R, 2001). I'd also like to mention

77

the work of contemporary Catholic author William K. McDonough, *The Divine Family: The Trinity and Our Life in God* (Cincinnati, OH: St. Anthony Messenger Press, 2005).

4. For instance, Millard J. Erickson, in his classic work *Christian Theology*, formally defines adoption as a "declarative matter, an alteration of our legal status." See Millard J. Erickson, *Christian Theology* (Grand Rapids, MI: Baker, 1998), 975. I have a tremendous amount of respect for Dr. Erickson, but while adoption certainly includes both declarative and legal realities, these are only applied to believers as a result of being personally united to Christ. Therefore, one could rightly say that the gift of adoption is a legal and declarative matter, but *only* within the context of personally participating in the person of Jesus Christ, in whom all such benefits lie.

5. Packer, *Knowing God*, 182.

6. Clark Pinnock, quoted in Veli-Matti Kärkkäinen, *One with God* (Collegeville, MN: Liturgical Press, 2004), 85.

7. Fil Anderson, *Breaking the Rules: Trading Performance for Intimacy with God* (Downers Grove, IL: InterVarsity, 2010), 224.

8. Richard Rohr, *Everything Belongs: The Gift of Contemplative Prayer* (New York: Crossroad, 1999), 25. Emphasis in the original.

9. *The Complete Poetical Works of John Greenleaf Whittier*, ed. Horace E. Scudder (Boston and New York: Houghton Mifflin, 1894), 291.

**CHAPTER 8: THE SPIRITUAL DISCIPLINES: PARADIGM SHIFT**

1. Richard Rohr, *Everything Belongs: The Gift of Contemplative Prayer* (New York: Crossroad, 1999), 27.

2. Richard Foster, *Celebration of Discipline* (San Francisco: HarperOne, 2002), 7–8.

3. According to a 2013 poll taken by the American Bible Society, over 50 percent of American Christians read their Bibles four times a year or less. Close to 60 percent of churchgoing eighteen- to twenty-eight-year-olds stated they read their Bibles less than three times a year, if at all. See Caleb K. Bell, "Poll: Americans Love the Bible but Don't Read It Much," April 4, 2013, http://www.religionnews.com/2013/04/04/poll-americans-love-the-bible-but-dont-read-it-much/.

4. Watchman Nee, *Sit, Walk, Stand* (Carol Stream, IL: Tyndale, 1977), 2.

5. See *The Essential Tillich: An Anthology of the Writings of Paul Tillich*, ed. F. Forrester Church (Chicago: University of Chicago Press, 1999), 180.

6. Brennan Manning, *Abba's Child: The Cry of the Heart for Intimate Belonging* (Colorado Springs: NavPress, 2015), 39.

7. Joseph de Beaufort and Brother Lawrence, in *The Practice of the Presence of*

*God*, accessed October 27, 2015, at http://thepracticeofthepresenceofgod .com/onlinetext.

8. Rohr, *Everything Belongs*, 29.

9. Leighton Ford, *The Attentive Life: Discerning God's Presence in All Things* (Downers Grove, IL: InterVarsity, 2008), 12, emphasis added.

10. I snagged the play on words from Leighton Ford in *The Attentive Life*, 13.

11. Fil Anderson, *Running on Empty* (Colorado Springs: Waterbrook, 2005), 51.

12. I'm happy to say that through the miracle of medication, God has healed me of my depression and anxiety. Further, I have not experienced anxiety-induced vomiting since. I'm *beyond* grateful to God.

## CHAPTER 9: THE CHURCH: THE BODY OF CHRIST

1. Josh Packard and Ashleigh Hope, *Church Refugees* (Loveland, CO: Group, 2015).

2. Neil Carter, "The 'Nones' vs. the 'Dones,'" *Godless in Dixie* (blog), March 27, 2015, http://www.patheos.com/blogs/godlessindixie/2015/03/27/the -nones-vs-the-dones/.

3. Pierre Benoit, quoted in George Maloney, *The Mystery of Christ in You* (Staten Island, NY: Alba House, 1998).

4. Cyril of Alexandria, cited in Emile Mersch, *The Whole Christ: The Historical Development of the Doctrine of the Mystical Body in Scripture and Tradition*, trans. John R. Kelly (Milwaukee: Bruce Publishing, 1938), 326.

5. Martin Luther, *Lectures on Galatians* 1535, in *Luther's Works*, vol. 26 (Philadelphia: Fortress, 1957), 168.

6. John Calvin, *Institutes of the Christian Religion*, 4.17, ed. John T. McNeill, trans. Ford Lewis Battles, Library of Christian Classics, vols. 20–21 (Philadelphia: Westminster, 1960), 351–352.

7. Augustus Strong, quoted in Marcus Peter Johnson, *One with Christ: An Evangelical Theology of Salvation* (Wheaton, IL: Crossway, 2013), 56.

8. Calvin, *Institutes of the Christian Religion*, 1. Emphasis added.

9. Again, during the Nestorian controversy the early church fathers insisted that the Son of God *had* to fully unite himself with humanity in order for humanity to be healed of its sin.

10. See Martin Luther, "Instructions to the Perplexed and Doubting, To George Spenlein, April 8, 1516," in Theodore G. Tappert, ed., *Luther: Letters of Spiritual Counsel*, Library of Christian Classics (Louisville, KY: Westminster John Knox, 1955), 110.

11. Luther, "Instructions to the Perplexed and Doubting," 110.

12. See Philippians 2:5-11. When Ephesians 5:25 is read in context, we see that

Christ cleanses the church in himself through "the washing of water with the word, so that he might present the church to himself in splendor, without spot or wrinkle or any such thing, that she might be holy and without blemish" (Ephesians 5:26-27).

13. Some evangelicals are suspicious of the word *Eucharist* (from the Greek *eucharistia*, meaning "thanksgiving"). While sounding Catholic or Orthodox, it has a rich history of use in Protestant evangelicalism. Martin Luther, John Calvin, A. W. Tozer, C. S. Lewis, John Stott, and Billy Graham have all employed the word in both writing and worship. I hope that contemporary evangelicalism can recapture the beauty and wonder of this word. But in order not to distract, I will use the more familiar word *Communion* or the phrase "the Lord's Supper."

14. For many evangelicals, the idea of Christ's presence in the Lord's Supper is a bit foreign. Yet for the first seventeen hundred years of the church, Christ's real presence in the Supper was seen as commonplace. See Donald Fairbairn, *Life in the Trinity: An Introduction to Theology with the Help of the Church Fathers* (Downers Grove, IL: InterVarsity, 2009), 210–219. While disagreements occurred (as they do today) as to how literally to understand Christ's presence in the Supper, the early church (per Paul) insisted that somehow Christ himself was really and truly present in the Communion meal (see 1 Corinthians 10:16). Fairbairn, drawing on the witness of the early church fathers, provides a much needed reminder as to the mind-set of the early church regarding Communion: "Just as the early church submitted to Scripture without articulating a doctrine of Scripture, and just as the Fathers directed their faith toward Christ without explaining clearly what was and was not faith, so also here, the Fathers insisted that the Eucharist points us to Christ and enables us to feed on him, without seeing the need to define with any specificity how that can be possible" (p. 218).

15. It's important to note that the Incarnation is a one-time-and-forever act in which the Son of God fully assumed a human nature that he will never jettison. Therefore, in the words of Robert Letham, "Christ is at the right hand of the Father, qua his humanity, and so he is in one place." Yet through the ordained elements of bread and wine, the Holy Spirit, in the words of John Calvin, "joins things separated by distance" allowing Christians to really and truly commune with the incarnate Christ through the Eucharist. See Robert Letham, *Union with Christ: In Scripture, History, and Theology* (Phillipsburg, NJ: P&R Publishing, 2011), 112, 125–126.

16. John Calvin, *Institutes of the Christian Religion*, 4.14, ed. John T. McNeill, trans. Ford Lewis Battles, Library of Christian Classics, vols. 20-21

(Philadelphia: Westminster, 1960), 16, as quoted by Leonard J. Vander Zee in Marcus Peter Johnson, *One with Christ: An Evangelical Theology of Salvation* (Wheaton, IL: Crossway, 2013), 216.

17. Coined by Leonard J. Vander Zee. Taken from Johnson, *One with Christ*, 216.

## CHAPTER 10: THE MISSION OF CHRIST: SO THAT THE WORLD MAY KNOW

1. There is some speculation as to whether "the disciple Jesus loved" was really John. Some biblical scholars suggest that it might have been Lazarus. I don't really have a dog in the fight. If it was John, awesome. If it was Lazarus, fantastic. For an interesting article on this see Ben Witherington, "Was Lazarus the Beloved Disciple?" January 29, 2007, http://benwitherington.blogspot.com/2007/01/was-lazarus-beloved-disciple.html.
2. David Kinnaman and Gabe Lyons, *UnChristian* (Grand Rapids: Baker, 2007), 27.
3. See Matthew 25:31-46; Luke 10:25-37; Luke 14:13-14; James 2:1-17. It was out of the self-giving, other-oriented love between the Father, Son, and Spirit that the Holy Three intentionally chose to share *their* love for one another with the world. In the same way, Christians, sharing in the life and love of the Trinity, are called to love the world out of their love for one another as the body of Christ.
4. Sandra Toenies Keating, "*Nostra Aetate* and Christian Witness," National Workshop on Christian Unity, Charlotte, North Carolina, April 21, 2015.
5. C. S. Lewis, *The Four Loves* (Boston: Mariner Books, 1971), 65.
6. It's interesting that in 1 Corinthians 1:10-17, Paul characterizes the disunion of the church in Corinth as causing "the cross of Christ [to] be emptied of its power" (1:17). Sobering.
7. John Murray, *Redemption Accomplished and Applied* (Grand Rapids: Eerdmans, 1955), 161.

# IS AN IMPOSTOR ROBBING YOU OF GOD'S LOVE?

"Honest. Genuine. Creative. God-hungry. These words surface when I think of the writings of Brennan Manning. Read him for yourself—you'll see what I mean!"

Max Lucado, New York Times bestselling author

AVAILABLE AT NAVPRESS.COM
OR WHERE CHRISTIAN BOOKS ARE SOLD.

CP0914